THE BATTLE

THE BATTLE

Let the Lord Fight Your Battle

Dr. Norris D. Hall

TheBattle

Copyright © 2019 by Dr. Norris D. Hall. All rights reserved.

No part of this publication may be reproduced, stored in a retrieval system or transmitted in any way by any means, electronic, mechanical, photocopy, recording or otherwise without the prior permission of the author except as provided by USA copyright law.

The opinions expressed by the author are not necessarily those of URLink Print and Media.

1603 Capitol Ave., Suite 310 Cheyenne, Wyoming USA 82001
1-888-980-6523 | admin@urlinkpublishing.com

URLink Print and Media is committed to excellence in the publishing industry.

Book design copyright © 2019 by URLink Print and Media. All rights reserved.

Published in the United States of America
ISBN 978-1-64367-810-8 (Paperback)
ISBN 978-1-64367-809-2 (Digital)

03.09.19

Dedication

This book is dedicated to my husband, Alfonza, who has given me many years of love, companionship and support. Thank you for being by my side through my trials.

I also dedicate this book to the memory of my father, the late Mr. Willie D. Davis, to my mother, the late Mrs. Alice Davis. I dedicate this book to my sisters, Eva D. Ferguson and Linda A. Wallace, to my four brothers, Bobby, Melvin, Willie and Carl, to my Pastor, Rev. Carlton Carlington. Thanks also to Michelle Jackson; I will always appreciate your love and support.

I also want to acknowledge the compassion and encouragement that I consistently received from my church family.

Contents

Introduction 9
Let The Lord Fight Your Battle 11
God Will Deliver 13
Suffering For Christ 30
This Bitter Cup 39
The Just Shall Live By Faith 47
The Valley Of The Shadow Of Death 54
Let God Be The Judge 63
The Rapture 71
Don't Waste The Grace 81
Being Rejected In Your Community 90
The Battle 103
I Will Bless The Lord At All Times 120
Praying For Results 128
Praying Without Ceasing 143
The Lord Is Merciful 161
Endnotes 173

INTRODUCTION

No matter how bad the condition of your life or your mind may be, do not give up! Take back all the things the devil has stolen from you. Whatever you may be facing or experiencing right now in your life, I am encouraging you to go through it and not give up! You must remember Jesus did not give up on you. So do not give up on Him. When the battle seems endless and you think you will never make it, when you face towering problems and you do not know what to do, have faith and trust in God. He will bring you through. Recall how God has helped you in the past. Read God's Holy Word. Reading and staying in His Holy Word gives you strength to carry on.

The Apostle Paul encourages us to keep on keeping on! Do not be a quitter! Do not have that spirit of giving up. God is looking for people who will go all the way with Him.

Take heart because God gives you strength. Use the skills God has already given you and move forward, remember that the battle is not yours, **it is the LORD'S**.

LET THE LORD FIGHT YOUR BATTLE

At the age of thirty, my calling to preach came to me in a dream, a strange man said, "Let God Be the Judge. Many will try to deceive you by telling you God did not call you to preach. You Let God Be The Judge. When I awoke from that dream, I could not believe it. I thought to myself, Is God calling me to preach? A shy county girl like me could not be a preacher. This recurring dream haunted me for three and a half years. It was if I could not run from it.

The stranger in my dreams told me to read John 22:17: *Jesus saith unto her, Touch me not; for I am not yet ascended to my Father; but go to my brethren, and say unto them, I ascend unto my Father, and your Father, and to my God, and your God.* Jesus gave Mary Magdalene the task of spreading the good news. The good news of His Glorious resurrection and His ascending back to God. Mary thought she was there to visit Christ's tomb, but Jesus redirected her task and she became the first female evangelist.

I was born into a God fearing family; there is no surprise to my acceptance of Jesus Christ. At an early age, I loved and believed in God. I always played the preacher when I played church with my brothers and sisters.

The first test of my faith was during the illness of my brother. I believed God for the healing of my brother on whom the doctors had given up. God healed his body and recruited a prayer warrior on the battlefield in me, Little Norris Davis. I began praying for others and later accepted the calling on my life as a pastor. I administer

Dr. Norris D. Hall

God's words to dying souls and preach the power of prayer to all. I previously published a book, "The Power of Prayer" in 2008. I am the Pastor of New Piney Grove in Eastman, GA and the Chaplin of the Georgia Bureau of Investigations.

God Will Deliver

When I was a little girl, my Mother told me my Granddaddy always said, "God got a calling on her life. She's going to be something one day."

My sisters and brothers played the usual children's games. However, I always wanted to play church. I always wanted to be the preacher. I recall playing church one day and we had a funeral. We took a doll and put it in a box. I preached the funeral and I used as a theme, "Jesus Wants Some Children in Heaven." At the age of ten, I was teaching Sunday school. I wanted to learn more and more about Jesus. [*Matthew 19:13-14: Then were there brought unto Him little children that He should put His hands on them, and pray; and the disciples rebuked them. vs14. But Jesus said, "Suffer little children, and forbid them not, to come unto me: for of such is the Kingdom of heaven."*] Christ is deeply concerned abut the salvation and the spiritual up-bringing of children. Christian parents should use every means of grace available to bring their children to Christ. He longs to receive them, love them, and bless them.

At the age of nine, I received Christ as my Lord and Savior and God as my heavenly Father and was baptized. As a child, I wanted to get to know more about Jesus. I wanted to fellowship with Him. I wanted Him to lead me and walk with me. As a child, I did not understand so many things about Jesus. Therefore, I prayed for understanding.

At the age of twelve, I formed a youth choir. I was president of the missionary and sang in the choir. Anything I could do in the church, I did it. I always walked in the light so other young women could see Jesus in me. I grew up in a loving family of four brothers and two sisters and I was the oldest. When they got sick, I always prayed for them. As a child, I heard a preacher preach a sermon about prayer and how prayer changes things. I heard my mother talk about prayer is the way we talk to God. Pray with faith. God will do what you ask of Him. Then I wanted to know what faith was. My mother said, "when you pray; go on and thank God for it. You know it is fixed." [*Hebrews 11:1: now faith is the substance of things hoped for, the evidence of things not seen.*]

Growing up, my mother told us not to be ashamed of the Gospel of Christ. I have always been a very shy person, but when I am speaking about Jesus, I can speak **BOLDLY**. When I was 28, I became sickly. I began to stay on my knees and pray because I knew that prayer would change things. Now I know how to stay in the Word of God. I learned how to pray without ceasing. [*1 Thessalonians 5:17-18: Pray without ceasing. In everything, give thanks: for this is the will of God in Christ Jesus concerning you.*] This means to abide in the presence of the Father, having a continual cry from the heart for His grace and blessing. [*Romans 12:12: Rejoicing in hope; patient in tribulation; continuing instant in prayer*] [*St. Luke 18:1: And He spake a parable unto them to this end, that men ought always to pray, and not to faint.*]

Jesus was frequently concerned that His followers pray continually in order to accomplish God's will for their lives. Moreover, I surely wanted to be in God's will. As the years passed, I began to feel like the woman that had the issue of blood for twelve long years. She spent all her money on doctors and none could heal her. [*St. Luke 8:43*] I did not give up. I kept the faith. I kept praying. I was having back problems. I ended up having three back surgeries, two of which were eighteen days apart. Reality is important to remember that for every person there will be a problem. Even more important, for every problem, God has a prescription.

I was suffering because of something that attacked me in the past. Although, the problem may have been rooted in the past, the prescription **is** a present Word from God! The Word is the same yesterday, today and for evermore. [*Hebrew 13:2*]

My problem did not begin suddenly. It existed from birth. I was a woman whom had a personal war going on inside of her. These struggles tainted many other areas of my life. I kept faith that I would be well one day. I did not give up. I kept praying. My mother kept praying. My husband kept praying. Even my church family kept praying. I knew that Jesus loved me and I was covered under His blood. He had not turned His back on me. God is Love. God proved His love not by His need of us, but by His giving to us. [*For God so loved the world, that he gave his only begotten Son, that whosoever believeth in him should not perish, but have everlasting life. John 3:16*]

[*But, let all those that put their trust in thee rejoice: let them ever shout for joy, because thou defendest them: let them also that love thy name be joyful in thee. Psalm 5:11*] When I awake every morning, I remember that scripture.

I wake up in the middle of the night thinking to myself, "If I can just get close enough to touch His garment." The devil was trying to steal my joy. [*Submit yourselves, therefore, to God. Resist the devil, and he will flee from you. James 4:7*]

For those who are suffering and hurting, God has intensive care. There will be a time in your life when God nurtures you through crisis. You may not even realize how many times God has intervened to relieve the tensions and stresses of daily living.

Every now and then, God does us a favor. He does something we did not earn or cannot even explain; we can only accept it as the loving hand of God. He knows when the load is overwhelming. Many times God moves (it seems to us) just in the knick of time.

When I was sick, surgery after surgery, I thought about when Jesus called a woman who was crippled and bent over. [*Luke 13:13*] She had come to church and sat in the synagogue for years and nobody helped her until Jesus saw her. When we can see someone else overcome a handicap, it helps us to overcome. [*Jesus said, "Come unto Me, all ye that labour and are heavy laden, and I will give you rest." Matthew 11:28*]

Early one morning, after eight years of back problems, God said, "I am going to deliver you and heal you. Now I am going to renew you and release you. I am going to tell you who you really are. Now I am ready to reveal to you why you had to go through what you did to become what you shall become. Just realize that you are the daughter of a King. Your Father is the King."

When the woman with the issue of blood came behind Jesus and touched the border of his garment, immediately her issue of blood stanched and [*Jesus asked, "Who touched me?" When all denied, Peter and they that were with him said, "Master, the multitude throng thee and press thee, and sayest thou, who touched me?" Jesus said, "Somebody hath touched me, for I perceive that the virtue is gone out of me." And when the woman saw that she was not hid, she came trembling, and falling down before him, she declared unto him before all the people for what caused she had touched him, and how she was healed immediately. And He said unto her, "Daughter, be of good comfort: thy faith hath made thee whole; go in peace. Luke 8:45-48*] For the first time in eight years, I was healed! When you come to Jesus, He will cause you to stand in His strength. You will know how important you are to Him. All I had to do was allow His power and anointing to touch the hurting places. He restored me. He built me back up.

I could not walk at one point. He delivered me by the power of His Spirit. [*Not by might, nor by power, but by my Spirit, saith the Lord of Hosts. Zechariah 4:6*] The anointing of the living God reached out to me. He called me forth and set me free. I was still praying and keeping the faith. So I began to fast. My mother always told me to fast and pray: to humble my soul before God.

Every night I dreamed I was reading Luke 4:18: THE SPIRIT OF THE LORD IS UPON ME, BECAUSE HE HATH ANOINTED ME TO PREACH THE GOSPEL TO THE POOR. HE HATH SENT ME TO HEAL THE BROKENHEARTED, TO PREACH DELIVERANCE TO THE CAPTIVES, AND RECOVERING OF SIGHT TO THE BLIND, TO SET AT LIBERTY THEM THAT ARE BRUISED.

I had thought that I would never rejoice again. But, God declares that I can have freedom in Him! He identifies with my pain and suffering. He knows what it is like to suffer. I cannot change where I have been, but I can change where I am going. [*Lift up your heads, O ye gates; even lift them up, ye everlasting doors; and the King of glory shall come in. Who is this King of glory? The Lord of Hosts, He is the King of glory. Selah. Psalm 24:9*]

All my life, I have had a tremendous compassion for hurting and suffering people. When other people would put their foot on them, I always tended to have a word of mercy. Perhaps it is because I have had my own pain. When you have suffered, it makes you able to relate to other people's pain. I learned how to put my trust in Jesus Christ, how to have faith and lean on Him. He did not come every time I called Him or prayed to Him, but he was always on time.

[Now Martha said to Jesus, "Lord, if you had been here, my brother would not have died. But even now, I know that whatever you ask of God, God will give you." John 11:21-22]. We see the faith of Martha in connection with the resurrection of her brother, Lazarus. Now Lazarus fell ill, and Martha and her sister, Mary, sent for Jesus to come and heal him. Jesus delayed His coming until Lazarus was dead and had been in the tomb for four days. When He came to raise him from the dead, he found the limited, fundamental faith of Martha His only obstacle. Martha's faith was limited. She said, "Lord, if you had been here, my brother would not have died." The death of Lazarus meant the end of Martha's faith. She believed that Jesus had the power to raise her brother up from the sick-bed, but not from the dead. Her limited faith restricted the power of Christ. Fear of failure in our circumstances limits faith.

Martha's faith was fundamental. Jesus said, "Your brother will rise again." These words were spoken to kindle hope and faith in Martha; but she said, "I know that he will rise again on the day of resurrection." Martha declared her fundamental faith in a great truth, but that is not enough…Jesus stated, "I am the resurrection and the life." Jesus was saying that He had all power over life and death. Then He asked, "Do you believe this?" Martha evaded the question by stating her fundamental faith in her creed.

It is not enough to believe in a creed only; faith must go beyond your creed to the living, all-powerful Christ. Her faith limited the power of Christ and "Jesus wept." Jesus wept when He came to raise Lazarus from the dead and found limited, fundamental faith only.

At last, unlimited faith came to Martha when she consented to have the stone moved from the grave. When Jesus first ordered the stone taken from the grave, Martha objected in unbelief. Then Jesus, challenging her to believe, said, "Did I not say to you that if you would believe you would see the glory of God?" Martha believed and waited to see the glory of God, and she was not disappointed. We often hear that "seeing is believing" but this is not so. You believe and then see. Faith comes before sight.

Martha's faith no longer limited the power of Christ. She consented to have the stone moved from the tomb and Jesus "cried with a loud voice, 'Lazarus, come forth!'" and Lazarus was raised up. Do not be satisfied with limited, fundamental faith only, when you can have unlimited faith that pleases God and reveals His glory.

At the age of thirty, my calling to preach came to me in a dream. In a dream, a strange man said, "Let God be the Judge. Many will try to deceive you by telling you women are not supposed to preach. You let God be the Judge. Use that as a subject." When I awoke from that dream, I could not believe it. God called me to preach! A shy, country girl like me could not be a preacher. I thought, "Let me pray about this."

This recurring dream haunted me for three and a half years. It was as if I could not run from it. I still did not know what to do. I knew I loved the Lord and I wanted to work in His vineyard. However, my preaching was not an option. I began singing in the choir. I taught Sunday school and I spoke in different churches on various programs. Looking back, that was God's way of preparing me for my destiny to preach.

Even though I was working faithfully in the vineyard, it was not what God required of me. I did everything but preach. I just did not want to stand before a crowd of people and preach. I kept running and I kept dreaming. That same stranger in my dream directed me to the scriptures, John 8:15-16: *ye judge after the flesh; I judge no man. And yet if I judge, my judgment is true: for I am not alone, but I and the Father that sent me.* He said, "Let God be the Judge." Jesus judges no man after the flesh. When we judge, we judge after the flesh. Our judgments are limited because we simply do not have all the facts. The Lord Jesus gives the judgment that comes from heaven. God's viewpoints are all that matters.

Still, I just could not face the music. I just could not see my self standing before a crowd and preaching God's Holy Words. I was still running and dreaming. The stranger in my dreams told me to read John 22:17: *Jesus saith unto her, Touch me not; for I am not yet ascended to my Father; but go to my brethren, and say unto them, I ascend unto my Father, and your Father; and to my God, and your God.*

Jesus gave Mary Magdalene the task of spreading the good news. The good news of His Glorious resurrection and His ascending back to God. Mary thought she was there to visit Christ's tomb, but Jesus redirected her task and she became the first female evangelist. Mary changed from a fearing, hopeless woman to a faithful, testifying disciple. The difference and change made was the presence of Jesus. She had seen Jesus, not the disciples. The disciples went home. She stayed.

Finally, I told my husband about the recurring dream. I told him I had been dreaming the Lord was calling me to preach. He did not question me. He told me if the Lord is calling you to preach I will be with you one hundred percent of the way.

One weekend, we went fishing with my husband's Pastor and his wife. My husband and I were members of different churches at this time. I told them about God calling me to preach. They both accepted my calling and said they would stand behind me all the way.

I kept praying. I kept trusting and believing in God. I knew this task was not going to be easy. I was a member of a Baptist Church and I did not know of any female ministers within the Baptist Association at this time. I began hearing the negative talk. Friends, or so-called friends, began turning their backs on me. I knew it was not going to be easy.

I dreamed yet another dream about my calling. This person came to me in my dream and told me the battle was not mine. He also told me that I HAD TO SUFFER AS Christ suffered. He said

I would have trials and tribulations. I thought to myself, "Not me Lord. I am not that strong."

After much consideration, prayers, fasting and trusting in the Lord, I decided to tell my Pastor that the Lord had called me to preach. He said to me, "I am with you, but no one else in the Baptist Church will be for you." Then he said, "If God be for you, who can be against you? Greater is He that is in you, than He that is in the world. 1 John 4:4v."

All my life, I heard women were not supposed to preach. As God dealt with my spirit about preaching, I decided to study the Bible and read for myself to see if God really said women are not to preach. I studied and studied the Words of God. I did not find anything that stated women are not to preach. People began telling me I cannot preach. They began to tell me women are not supposed to preach. God meant for women to keep silent in the church. I thought to myself," No way that can be true."

Although I was being told a woman is not to preach, no one could tell me *why not* nor show me in the Bible the reason a woman could not spread God's Word. Those small-minded people based their theory on 1 Corinthians 14:34-35 [vs. 34 Let your women keep silence in the churches for it is not permitted unto them to speak; but they *are commanded* to be under obedience, as also saith the law. 35 And if they will learn anything, let them ask their husbands at home: for it is a shame for women to speak in the church.]

I studied, prayed, and asked God to open up these two scriptures to me. Help me, Lord, to understand just what Paul is saying. If women kept silent in the church, there would be no church. More women attend church than men do. If the only way women can learn is by asking their husbands at home, how will the women who are not married learn? How will they learn? I kept studying and praying to God to show me what 1 Corinthians 14: 34-35 was truly saying.

There was a church meeting at Corinth. In those days, most women were uneducated. The assembling of believers was not a place for women asking questions. They even prohibited questions about spiritual matters. Instead, they told them to ask their husbands at home. In understanding Paul's instructions in context, he wanted order and harmony in church meetings. Talking women would be a distraction. Unnecessary talking should not take place in a meeting of the believers that gather to worship God.

Paul was not saying women could not preach. He only called for order in the meetings. Further down in the scriptures, Paul says in the 37th verse if "ANY" man thinks himself to be a prophet, or spiritual, let him acknowledge that the things that I write unto you are the commandments of the Lord.

Paul removes all ethnic, racial, national, social, and sexual distinctions with regard to one's spiritual relationship with Jesus Christ. All in Christ are equal heirs of the grace of life, the Promised Spirit and renewal in the image of God. This truth is emphasized in the scripture, in the 3rd chapter and 28th verse of the book of Galatians: *There is neither Jew nor Greek, there is neither bond nor free, there is neither male nor female; for ye are all one in Christ Jesus.*

Everything done in worship services must be beneficial to the worshippers. Every worshiper ought to consider himself or herself a contributor. These principles touch every aspect—singing, preaching, and the exercising of spiritual gifts. Contributions to the service (by singing, speaking, reading, praying, playing instruments, giving) must have love as their chief motivation. As you prepare to lead or participate in worship, seek to strengthen the faith of other believers.

And if they will learn any thing, let them ask their husband at home: for it is a shame for women to speak in the church (1 Cor. 25:35). Does this mean that women should not speak in church services today? It is clear from verse 1 Corinthians 11:15 that women prayed and prophesied in public worship. It is clear in chapters 1 Corinthians 14:34-35 that women are given spiritual gifts and are encouraged to exercise them in the body of Christ. Women have much to contribute and can participate in worship services.

Women can be schoolteachers, doctors, lawyers, construction workers, scientists, even athletes, and society accepts it. They can even run for President of the United States! However, when a woman has a calling to preach, the world has a problem with it. Not so much the world, but Satan, has the problem with it. [*Ephesians 6:12: for we wrestle not against flesh and blood, but against principalities, against powers, against the rulers of darkness of this world, against spiritual wickedness in high places.*]

Now, my trial sermon began to approach. My pastor said, "I would talk with the Chairman of the church and see what he says about you preaching your trial sermon at this church." I thought to myself, "Lord, you called me. You fix it for me." The Chairman of the church had already said, "No woman was going to preach in this church!" That was what *he* said. **God said**, "Put me in remembrance; let us plead together; declare thou, that thou mayest be justified" (Isaiah 43:26 v). God invites us to remind Him of His Word. When we remind God of His Word, we are just calling His attention to what He has already promised us. [*The Lord shall fight for you and ye shall hold your peace. Exodus 14:14*]

My Pastor at that time talked to the Chairman of the church. He asked him if I could preach my trial sermon in this church. The Chairman did not tell the Pastor anything. However, the Chairman called me the next morning and said, "You can preach your trial sermon here." I preached my trial sermon the 1st Sunday in November of 1995 in the very church that kicked against me, a female preacher!

[*Rejoicing in hope; patient in tribulation, continuing instant in prayer; Romans 12:12*] By now, I had faith in my calling. I knew God had called me to preach. I heard the voice of the Lord saying, "Whom shall I send, and who will go for us?" Then I said, "I. Here am I. Send me."

The time came for my licensing by the church. Everybody was saying, "The church is not going to license a woman to preach." I told the Lord, "This is your battle; you did not bring me this far to leave me now." Everybody was in an uproar, saying, "God did not tell a woman to preach." I stayed in the background and watched God work on my behalf. Two weeks from the day I preached my trial sermon, I received my license.

On top of all that, my Pastor, who was with me through all the drama, resigned the night of my licensing. I thought to myself, "Lord what now?" That night, I dreamed that the Lord was telling me to lean and depend on Him. He told me, "I would not let you down." It seemed as though many people were fighting against me just because I said that God called me to preach. He also told me that I had to suffer trials and tribulations just as He did. Again, I thought, "No, not me Lord." [*Say to them that are of a fearful heart, be strong, fear not: behold, your God will come with vengeance, even God with a recompense; he will come and save you. Isaiah 35:4*]

Beloved, think it not strange concerning the fiery trial which is to try you as though some strange thing happened unto you: but rejoice, inasmuch as ye are partakers of Christ's sufferings; that, when his glory shall be revealed, ye may be glad also with exceeding joy. If ye be reproached for the name of Christ, happy are ye; for the spirit of glory and of God resteth upon you: on their part he is evil spoken of, but on your part he is glorified (1 Peter 4: 12- 14). Trouble was breaking loose on every side in my life and I thought I could not take it anymore, but God intervened and broke every chain that held me back. I had a husband and a mother who stood by my side. I never stopped praying. I knew that I had to keep the faith. [*But without faith it is impossible to please Him; for he that cometh to God must believe that He is, and that He is a rewarder of them that diligently seek Him. Hebrews 11:6 v.*]

God will reward those who persevere in seeking Him. He may not come when you want Him to, but He is always on time. If you will wait on the Lord, He will strengthen your heart. He will heal you and deliver you. He will lift you up and break those chains. God's power will loose the bands from around your neck. He will give you the "garment of Praise for the spirit of heaviness" (Isaiah 61:3).

The enemy wanted to multiply fear in my life. Everybody was talking about "that woman preacher." Not only were the men fighting me, but the women were also. [*For God hath not given me the spirit of fear; but of power and of love, and of a sound mind 2 Timothy 1:7*].

Nothing hurts as much as a wound from a friend. At times friends may need to lovingly confront you in order to help you, but betrayal truly hurts. Betrayal by friends has caused me great anguish. Real friends stick by you in times of trouble and bring healing, love, acceptance, and understanding.

When the angel came to Mary and told her what God was going to do in her life, Mary questioned how it could be possible (Luke 1:34). Perhaps God has been telling you things He wants to do in your life, but you have questioned Him like Mary and I did. If you have been wondering how God will make things come to pass in your life, remember that He will accomplish the task.

He told Mary, "The Holy Ghost shall come upon thee." I believe the same is true of godly women today. The Holy Spirit will fill you. God had a special plan for Mary. She brought forth Jesus. He has a special plan for us.

After the angel told Mary those words, do you know what she said? "And Mary said, Behold the handmaid of the Lord; be it unto me according to thy word. And the angel departed from her" (Luke 1:38). Mary knew enough to believe God and to submit to Him. She was taking an extreme risk. To be pregnant and unmarried brought dire consequences in those days. Yet she willingly gave herself over to the Lord.

Mary had a cousin named Elizabeth who was already expecting a child. The child in Elizabeth's womb was to be the forerunner of Jesus. The two women came together to share their stories. When Elizabeth found a woman who would build her up the Bible says that the baby "leaped in her womb and she was filled with Holy Ghost" (Luke 1:41).

The things you had stopped believing God for will start leaping in your spirit again once you start trusting Him. God will renew you. Often times, women work against each other but God has a plan to bring us together. We will come together like Mary and Elizabeth. Every "Mary" needs an "Elizabeth." He wants us to come together and help each other.

The Church that I was a member of went against me. All the sisters in the church went against me. They said just because God called me to preach that I was tearing up the church. I said to them," Stop your wars and fighting. Throw down your swords and put away your shields. God put something in me that you need. When you come together, powerful things will happen."

Satan attempts to keep us from our potential. He causes horrible things to happen in our lives so those lives will take on a different outlook. There are great potentials in women who believe.

Although my Pastor resigned from the church, I was not on my own. It was God and me. The Lord was my leader. He guided me. He remained by my side.

I did not want to be the cause of confusion in the Church, so I asked God a question. "Lord, what do you want me to do?" That Sunday I went to a Gospel Singing. I was so burdened that I cried all the way there. After the Singing, an older man came out of the crowd and stood before me. Pointing his finger at me, he said, "God called you to preach. Get away from your people. God has many blessings for you. You got to move." It happened so quickly; and then he was gone. I just stood there in awe.

> *[Now the Lord had said unto Abram, get thee out of thy country, and from thy kindred, and from thy father's house, unto a land that I will show thee: And I will make of thee a great nation, and I will bless thee, and make thy name great; and thou shalt be a blessing; and I will bless them that bless thee, and curse him that curseth thee; and in thee shall all families of the earth be blessed. Genesis 12:1-3]*

This man came back a *second* time and pointed his finger at me and said, "The Lord said move. God wants to use you on the battlefield like He did Deborah". I went out like a light. When I regained consciousness, I asked who that man was. Everybody looked at me as if I had lost my mind. Nobody else saw this man. I believe that was my angel sent by God to tell me to move my membership from the Church that I was a member of so He can do wonders in my life. My mother told me to leave that church because God wanted to use me but He could not use me where I was. *[And Barak said unto her, If thou wilt go with me, then I will go: but if thou wilt not go with me, then I will not go. And she said, I will surely go with thee: notwithstanding the journey that thou takest shall not be for thine honour; for the Lord shall sell Sisera into the hand of a woman. And Deborah arose, and went with Barak to Kedesh. Judges 4:8-9]*

When the Lord gets through working on you, all your adversaries will be ashamed. You will not have to prove anything. God will prove it. When He gets through showing that you have done the right thing and come to the right place, they will drop their heads and be ashamed. Jesus let me know that I would have to go through trials just as He did. [*These things I have spoken unto you, that in me ye might have peace. In the world ye shall have tribulation: but be of good cheer; I have overcome the world. John 16:33*]

The religious critics did not like what Jesus had done. His power showed how powerless their religion was. The thing that moves God is FAITH. If you believe in Him, He will move in your life according to your faith and not to your experience. [*For ye are all the children of God by faith in Christ Jesus. Galatians 3:26*]

Women are just as much children of God as men. Everything that God will do for a man, He will do for a woman. [*There is neither Jew nor Greek, there is neither bond nor free, there is neither male nor female: for ye are all one in Christ Jesus. Galatians 3:28*]. God does not look at your gender; He looks at your heart. He does not look at morality or good works. He looks at the faith that lives within. God is looking in your heart. All people are one in Christ Jesus.

I left the church that held my membership. It was hard. I had been a member of that church since I was eight years old. I joined the church with my husband, where everyone welcomed me warmly. I served there as Associate Pastor. Then I decided to go back to school to get a Doctor of Ministry as well as my Doctor of Theology. Still, many places have not accepted me as a Pastor. [*So that we may boldly say,* **THE LORD IS MY HELPER, AND I WILL NOT FEAR WHAT MAN SHALL DO UNTO ME.** *Hebrews 13:6*]

It is easy to lose heart and quit. We all have faced problems in our relationships or work that have caused us to think about giving up. Rather than quitting when persecution ware you down, I had to concentrate on the inner strength that came from the Holy Spirit. Don't let fatigue, pain, or criticism force you off your job. Renew your commitment to serving Christ. Don't forsake your eternal reward because of the intensity of today's pain. Your very weakness allows the resurrection power of Christ to strengthen you moment by moment.

Our troubles ["light affliction"] should not diminish our faith or disillusion us. We should realize that there is a purpose in our suffering. Problems and human limitations have several benefits: (1) They remind us of Christ's suffering for us; (2) they keep us from pride; (3) they cause us to look beyond this brief life; (4) they prove our faith to others; and (5) they give God the opportunity to demonstrate his power. See your troubles as opportunities!

Our ultimate hope in terrible illness, persecution, or pain is realizing that this life is not all there is-there is life after death! Knowing that we will live forever with God in a place without sin and suffering can help us live above the pain we face in this life.

What a difference knowing Jesus can make! He cares for us in spite of what the world thinks. Christians don't have to give in to public opinion and pressure. Paul stood true to God whether people praised him or condemned him. He remained active, joyous, and content in the most difficult conditions. Don't let circumstances or people's expectations control you. Be firm as you stand true to God, and refuse to compromise his standards for living.

> *By honour and dishonor, by evil report and good report: as deceivers, and yet true; as unknown, and yet well known; as dying, and, behold, we live; as chastened, and not killed [Cor. 7:8-9].*

Everything done in worship services must be beneficial to the worshipers. Every worshiper ought to consider himself or herself a contributor. These principles touch every aspect-singing, preaching, and the exercise of spiritual gifts. Contributions to the service (by singing, speaking, reading, praying, playing instruments, giving) must have love as their chief motivation. As you prepare to lead or participate in worship, seek to strengthen the faith of other believers.

Does this mean that women should not speak in church service today? No, today women preach in church services. Women are given spiritual gifts and are encouraged to exercise them in the body of Christ. Women have much to contribute and can participate in worship services. There will always be people who say women are not to preach God Word. Just like there will always be people who say

Jesus didn't rise from the dead. Don't be discouraged by doubters who deny the resurrection. Be filled with hope because of the knowledge that one day you, and they, will see the living proof when Christ returns.

Many think that when God comforts us, our hardships should go away. But if that were always so, people would turn to God only to be relived of pain and not out of love for him. We must understand that *comfort* can also mean receiving strength, encouragement, and hope to deal with our hardships. The more we suffer the more comfort God gives us. If you are feeling overwhelmed, allow God to comfort you. Remember that every trial you endure will help you comfort other people who are suffering similar hardships.

The "sufferings of Christ" are those afflictions we experience for doing Christ's ministry. At the same time, Christ suffers in his people, as they are united with him. I remember in Acts 9:4, 5 Christ asked Paul why he was persecuting him. This implies that Christ suffered with the early Christians when they were persecuted. Suffering especially trials and discomfort associated with the advancement of Christ's Kingdom-is God's way of allowing Christians to become more like Jesus, to suffer for the Gospel just as Jesus suffered for it. Christians should rejoice when they suffer, for in their own suffering they will in some small way experience what it meant for Jesus to suffer for their sins.

In addition to drawing people closer to Christ, suffering can also help them in their faith. God uses suffering to improve his people and shape them into better Christians. In fact, suffering should be through of as the necessary pain that accompanies spiritual growth.

We often depend on our own skills and abilities when life seems easy, but when we feel unable to help ourselves, we turn to God. Depending on God is not defeat or weakness but a realization of our own powerlessness without him and our need for his constant contact. God is our source of power and we receive his help by keeping in touch with him. With this attitude, problems drive us to God rather away from him. Learn how to rely on God daily.

What a difference knowing Jesus can make! He cares for us in spite of what the world thinks. Christians do not have to give in to public opinion and pressure. Paul stood true to God whether people praised him or condemned him. He remained active, joyous, and content in the most difficult conditions. Don't let circumstances or people's expectations control you. I learn to be firm as I stand true to God, and refuse to compromise His standards for living.

SUFFERING FOR CHRIST

Jesus admonishes all believers to be constantly aware that the lost have an invaluable, everlasting soul and must spend eternity in heaven or in hell and that their salvation depends on someone presenting the gospel to them.

Those who willingly suffer for the cause of Christ find it easier to resist sin and to follow God's will. They have united themselves with Christ and shared His cross. As a result, the pull of sin is made insignificant and the will of God, permanent. This spiritual principle will work in the lives of all believers. Obeying God when it means suffering ridicule or rejection strengthens the believer morally and spiritually and one will receive from God a greater grace.

The highest glory and privilege of any believer is to suffer for Christ and the Gospel. In suffering, the believer follows the example of Christ and the apostles. Christians must be willing to share in the sufferings of Christ and expect suffering as a part of their ministry.

Suffering for Christ is called, "suffering according to the will of God", "suffering for His name's sake", "suffering for the Gospel", "suffering for righteousness' sake", and "suffering for the kingdom of God."

Suffering for Christ is a way to arrive at spiritual maturity, to obtain the blessing of God, and to minister life to others. Sharing in Christ's suffering is a prerequisite for glorification with Christ and attaining eternal "glory".

Jesus' prayer at Gethsemane was "heard" but not in the sense that God removed all that was involved in death, but in the sense that He received God's aid to undergo His "appointed" suffering. There will be times when we will face trials and our fervent prayers seem unanswered. In such times, we must remember that God tested Jesus' faith in the same way He tests our faith and God will give us sufficient grace to undergo what He allows to happen in our lives.

The eternal salvation obtained by the suffering of Jesus is available only to those who are obedient to Him through faith. *[And being made perfect, he became the author of eternal salvation unto all them that obey him. Hebrews 5:9].*

I can come **BOLDLY** unto the throne of grace because Christ sympathizes with my weaknesses. I can confidently approach the heavenly throne, knowing that my Heavenly Father welcomes and desires my prayers and petitions. His throne is the "throne of grace" because from it flows God's Grace. From it flows love, help, mercy, forgiveness, spiritual power, the outpouring of the Holy Spirit, His spiritual gifts, the fruit of the Holy Spirit, and all that we need under any circumstances. One of the greatest blessings of Salvation is that Christ is now our high priest opening a way to His personal presence whereby we can always seek the help we need.

[Notwithstanding, the Lord stood with me, and strengthened me; that by me the preaching might be fully known and that all the Gentiles might hear: and I was delivered out of the mouth of the lion. 2 Timothy 4:17]. The Lord stood with me because of the severe persecution against Baptist female ministers. I was deeply disappointed and felt deserted. However, in such times I experienced the Lord's special nearness as He stood by me and strengthened me.

A minister of the Gospel that remains loyal to Christ and the Gospel expects to endure hardship. Like a soldier, he or she must be willing to undergo difficulties and suffering and to wage spiritual warfare in wholehearted devotion to his or her Lord. Like an athlete, he or she must be willing to sacrifice and live a life of strict discipline. Like a farmer, he must be committed to hard work and long hours. *[If we suffer with him, we shall also reign with him; if we deny him, he also will deny us. 2 Timothy 2:12]*

Many church doors were closed in my face. I had to remember what Jesus went through when He was on this earth. My mother always told me, "When the Lord gets through working on you; all your adversaries will be ashamed. All your accusers will be ashamed of themselves. You will not have to prove anything. God will prove it."

God has called many women to preach His word, but they are afraid of what someone might say. Being a Baptist female preacher is not easy. I learned that trials and suffering only come to make us strong. One thing I had to learn was patience; I had to learn how to wait on Jesus. I had to learn how to glory the Lord in my tribulations.

Paul lists "tribulations" as one of the blessings of our salvation in Christ. The word "tribulation" refers to all kinds of trials which may press in upon us. This includes need, trying circumstances, the pressures of sorrow, sickness, persecution, mistreatment, or loneliness. I thought because God had called me to preach His Word everybody was going to accept me. Everybody was going to love me. How wrong I was! There are Pastors that will not even let women in their pulpit.

May I repeat my self "There is neither male nor female" (Gal. 3:28). God does not look at your gender. He looks at our heart. He does not look at morality and good works, He looks at faith that lives within, and all people are one in Christ Jesus. I had to keep praising God. The more they criticized me, the more I was justified because I just stood there and kept believing God. God was trying to get me to a place of faith. I have been brokenhearted many times; there are times I thought God had left me. I had to remember no matter how limited our earthly possessions may be or how trying our circumstances, I never need to fear that God will desert or forsake me. I learned to trust and lean on Jesus.

I have stood on the floor of many churches and preached the Word because I was not welcome in the pulpit. I learned that it does not matter where you stand; just preach the Word of God. Because I knew that the power and effect of God's Word are never canceled or rendered void; His Word will bring either spiritual life to those who receive it or just condemnation for those who reject it.

> *So shall my Word be that goeth forth out of my mouth: it shall not return unto me void, but it shall accomplish that which I please, and it shall prosper in the thing whereto I sent it [Isaiah 55:11].*

Jesus transformed Mary Magdalene into a strong woman. Mary totally dedicated herself to Jesus and His cause. Her faith was rewarded! Mary was among the first to hear of Jesus' resurrection, and she was the first to see and speak to the risen LORD. Forever stamped on the pages of sacred history is that it was not a man, but *Mary*, who was granted this great privilege. We can hardly doubt that Mary Magdalene, although overlooked by many who stressed the roles of Peter and John, was among the most faithful and honored disciples of Jesus Christ.

It is all too easy to be saved by Jesus and then go our own way. We are faithful when we need His help, but then our prayers lose their intensity.

Mary never seemed to lose her intensity. She was healed of demon possession, and from that point on, she never wavered in her commitment to Christ. Mary loved her LORD, not with a passion that would burn out, but with unceasing intensity.

It is fascinating that Jesus chose Mary to be the first to see Him after the resurrection and the first to share the Good News. It is curious: if Mary Magdalene were with us today, how many church pulpits would be closed to her? No matter how many hindrances to ministry may exist, no one can keep us from sharing Christ with neighbors and friends.

When I joined my husband's Church; everyone was so good to me. They welcomed me with open arms. The Devil tried to get some of the members to have the Pastor to put me out of the Church or take me out of the pulpit, the Pastor was great. He was a man of God. He always told me, "I don't know what God told nobody. I only know what he told me." I learned a lot from him. My Pastor always told me to keep praying, keep the faith: [*no weapon that is formed against thee shall prosper; ye are of God, little children, and have overcome them: because greater is he that is in you, than he that is in the world. 1 John 4:4*] I had to learn that God will let His children go through only so much, and then He will step in. God does not get excited about circumstances (Mark 4:39).

Another time, the disciples and Jesus were on a ship. The storm arose and appeared to be about to sink the ship. However, Jesus did not become concerned about circumstances. In fact, He was sleeping, resting in the middle of a crisis. Everyone else was running all over the boat trying to figure out how they would get into life jackets and into the lifeboats. Jesus was resting because He knew He was greater than the storm. Jesus rose up and spoke to the winds and waves and said, "Peace, be still" and the winds and waves *were stilled*.

When you know who you are, you do not have to struggle. I dare you to realize that you can do all things through Christ who strengthens you (Phil. 4:13).

I have learned to "never say never." Even I was one of them that said woman were not to preach. I did not know why; I had just heard everybody else saying that. I learned to let God be the JUDGE. I learned that God can and will use *anybody* that He wants to. If He can make a rock talk, if He can make a cock crow, you know He can use a woman. Previously, I would not go hear other women preach; I though that they were wrong. Again, I did not know why. I just heard somebody say it was wrong for a woman to preach and that she was not supposed to be the head of a man. When God called me to preach, He changed my outlook about women preachers. I have been knocked down to my knees, but every time I come back stronger. I learned that God's thoughts and ways are not those of the natural person. But human minds and hearts can be renewed and transformed by seeking Him; then our thoughts and ways will begin to conform to His. Our greatest desire should be to live in conformity to the likeness of our Lord that everything we do pleases the God we serve. We can do this by abiding in His word and responding to the leading of the Holy Spirit.

We will go through trials and persecutions, when we are in the midst of them, it make very little sense. But they can purify us if we are willing to learn from them. After you survive a difficult time, seek to learn from it so that it can help you in the future.

And not only so, but we glory in tribulations also: knowing that tribulation worketh patience [Romans 5:3].

This means we will experience difficulties that help us grow. "Glory in tribulations" means rejoicing in suffering. We rejoice in suffering, not because we like pain or deny its tragedy, but because we know God is using life's difficulties and Satan's attacks to build our character. The problems that we run into will develop our patience—which in turn will strengthen our character, deepen our trust in God, and give us greater confidence about the future. You probably find your patience tested in some way every day.

We can't really know the depth of our character until we see how we react under pressure. It is easy to be kind when everything is going well. But can we still be kind when others are treating us unfairly? God desires to make us mature and complete ("perfect"), not to keep us from all pain. Instead of complaining about our struggles, we should see them as opportunities for growth. I thank God for promising to be with me in rough times. All we have to do is ask him to help us solve our problems or give us the strength to endure them. Then be patient. God will not leave you alone with your problems; he will stay close by and help you grow.

> *My brethren, count it all joy when ye fall into divers temptations; knowing this, that the trying of faith worketh patience [James 1:2-3].*

James doesn't say if we face trials, but when we face them. He assumes we will have trials and that it is possible to profit from them. We are not required to pretend to be happy when we face pain, but to have a positive outlook because of the results trials will bring. James tells us to turn out hardships into times of learning. Tough times can teach us patient.

I have learned that the cross of Christ is a symbol of suffering, death, shame, ridicule, rejection, and self-denial. When we as believers take up our cross and follow Christ, we deny our own selves and commit ourselves to three areas of struggle and suffering:

(1) We suffer in a lifelong battle against sin by crucifying our own fleshly desires.
(2) We suffer in a war against Satan and the power of darkness as we advance the kingdom of God. We experience both the hostility of the adversary with his demonic host; and

the persecution which comes from standing against false teachers who distort the true.

(3) We suffer the reproach, hatred, and ridicule of the world by testifying in love that its deeds are evil, by separating ourselves from it both morally and spiritually, and by refusing to accept its standards or philosophy as our own.

(4) Like Jesus, we may also suffer ridicule and persecution from the religious world.

Whosoever therefore shall be ashamed of me and of my words in this adulterous and sinful shall the Son of man be ashamed, when he cometh in the glory of his generation; of him also Father with the holy angels [Mark 8:38].

Jesus sees the world and society in which we live as an "adulterous and sinful generation." All those who seek to be popular in or accepted by their present evil generation rather than follow Christ and His righteous standards, will be rejected by Christ at His return.

And lest I should be exalted above measure through the abundance of the revelations, there was given to me a thorn in the flesh, the messenger of Satan to buffet me, lest I should be exalted above measure. For this thing I besought the Lord thrice, that it might depart from me [2 Cor. 7-8].

We don't know what Paul's "thorn in the flesh" was, because he doesn't tell us. Some have suggested that it was malaria, epilepsy, or a disease of the eyes. Whatever it was, it was a chronic and debilitating problem, which at times kept him from working. This thorn was a hindrance to his ministry, and he prayed for its removal; but God refused. Paul was very self-sufficient person, so this thorn must have been difficult for him.

Three times Paul prayed for healing and did not receive it. He received, however, things far greater, because he received greater grace from God, a stronger character, humility, and an ability to empathize with others. In addition, it benefited those around him, as they saw God at work in his life. According to his sovereign plan, God doesn't heal some believers of their physical ailments. We do not know why some are spared and others are not. God chooses according to His divine purpose. Our task is to pray, believe, and trust. Paul is living proof that holy living and courageous faith do not ensure instant physical healing. When we pray for healing, we must trust our bodies to God's care. We must recognize that nothing separates us from his love and that our spiritual condition is always more important than our physical condition.

Although God did not remove Paul's affliction, he promised to demonstrate his power in Paul. The fact that God's power shows up in our weaknesses should give us courage. As we recognize our limitations, we will rely on God for our effectiveness rather then on our own energy, effort, or talent. Our limitations not only help develop Christian character, but also deepen our worship, because in admitting them, we affirm God's strength.

When we are strong in abilities or resources, we are tempted to do God's work on our own, and that can lead to pride. When we are weak, allowing God to fill us with his power, then we are stronger then we could ever be on our own. God does not intend for us to be weak, passive, or ineffective-life provides enough hindrances and setbacks without us creating them. When they come, we must depend on God. Only his power will make us effective for him and will help us do work that has lasting value.

Suffering helps us be like Christ, yet people will do anything to avoid pain. Followers of Christ, however, should be willing and prepared to do God's will and to suffer for it if necessary. We can overcome sin when we focus on Christ and what he wants us to do. Pain and danger reveal our true values. Anyone who suffers for doing good and still faithfully obeys in spite of suffering has made a clean break with sin.

The Holy Spirit gives Christians great power to live for God. Some Christians want more than this. They want to live in a state of perpetual excitement. The tedium of everyday living leads them to conclude that something is wrong spiritually. Often the Holy Spirit's greatest work in us is teaching us to persist, to keep on doing what is right even when it no longer seems new and interesting. If the Christian life seems ordinary, you may need the Spirit to stir up to see the challenge of everyday living. When trouble comes, don't be surprised.

It is not shameful to suffer for being a Christian. When Peter and John were persecuted for preaching the Good News, they rejoiced because such persecution was a mark of God's approval of their work. Don't seek out suffering, and don't try to avoid it. Instead, keep on doing what is right regardless of the suffering it might bring.

Carrying your worries, stress, and daily struggles by yourself shows that you have not trusted God fully with your life. It takes humility, however, to recognize that God cares, to admit your need, and to let others in your family help you. Sometimes we think that struggles caused by our own sin and foolishness are not God's concern. But when we turn to Him in repentance, He will bear the weight even of those struggles. Letting God have your worries is active, not passive. Don't submit to circumstances, but to the Lord, who controls circumstances.

When we are suffering, we feel as though our pain will never end. Peter shows these faithful Christians the wider perspective. In comparison with eternity, their suffering would last only "a while." Some of Peter's readers would be strengthened and delivered in their own lifetimes. Others would be released from their suffering through death. All of God's faithful followers are assured of an eternal life with Christ where there will be no suffering.

But the God of all grace, who hath called us unto His eternal glory by Christ Jesus, after that ye have suffered a while, make you perfect, stablish, strengthen, settle you [1 Peter 5:10].

THIS BITTER CUP

Say to them that are of a fearful heart, be strong, and fear not: behold, your God will come with vengeance, even God with a recompense; he will come and save you. Isaiah 35:4] God will one day come to recompense the world for its evil and to reward the righteous with His great salvation. At that time, the redeemed are saved from sin and its consequences.

As I think about how Jesus was treated, how He suffered, then I say, "Who am I?" [*For God so loved the world, that he gave his only begotten Son, that whosoever believeth in him should not perish, but have everlasting life. John 3:16]*

God "gave" His son as an offering for sin on the cross. The atonement proceeds from the loving heart of God. I would pray to God; I would say, "Lord, you called me to preach your Word. Why am I treated so badly? Why do I have to go through all this just to tell men and women, boys and girls about your word? Lord, why are some preachers treating me so meanly?" I had to learn a lot: not everybody that calls on the name of the Lord is saved. Jesus Christ went through so much for us. Why do some people get upset with me for telling them that Jesus loves them and He wants us to live in heaven with Him?

The physical and spiritual suffering of Christ begins in Gethsemane. His sweat was as if it were great drops of blood. Under great stress, the small capillaries in the sweat glands can break and mix blood with sweat. *[Then saith he unto them, My soul is exceeding sorrowful, even unto death: tarry ye here, and watch with me. And he went a little farther, and fell on his face, and prayed, saying, O my Father, if it be possible, let this cup pass from me: nevertheless not as I will, but as thou wilt. Matt. 26:38-39].*

What Christ meant by "this cup" has been the subject of much discussion. It is doubtful that Christ was praying to be saved from physical death, for He had resolutely set Himself to die for the sin of humankind. It is more probable that He was praying for deliverance from the punishment of separation from God the ultimate penalty for sin. Christ prayed that His physical death might be accepted as full payment for the sin of sinners. However, He prayed, "nevertheless, not as I will but as thou wilt." He then committed Himself to undergo both physical death and spiritual separation from His heavenly Father in order to achieve our salvation. His prayer was "heard," for He was strengthened by His Father to drink the appointed cup.

So I thought if Jesus Christ went through all that, I can go through for Him, who am I, going through my little suffering. The Roman scourge consisted of the victim being stripped and stretched against a pillar or bent over a low post, his hands being tied. The instrument of torture was a short wooden handle to which several leather thongs were attached, with bits of iron or bone tied to the thongs. The blows were laid on the victim's back by two men, one lashing the victim from one side, one from the other side. This resulted to the cutting of the flesh to such an extent those veins, arteries, and sometimes even inner organs, were exposed. Often the victim died during the flogging. The heavy beam of the cross was tied to Christ's shoulder. He began the slow journey to Golgotha. The weight of the wooden beam, together with sheer physical exhaustion, caused Him to fall. He tried to rise, but could not. Simon was then pressed into service to bear His cross. Then, I thought about what Jesus said in Luke 14:27, "And whosoever doth not bear his cross, and come after me, cannot be my disciple."

At Golgotha, the crossbeam was placed on the ground and Jesus was laid on it. His arms were stretched along the beams and a heavy, square, wrought- iron nail is driven through His hand (or wrist), first into the right, then into the left hand, and deep into the wood. Next, Christ was lifted up by means of ropes or ladders, the cross beam is bound or nailed to the upright beam, and a support for the body fastened on it. With His feet extended and a larger piece of iron driven through the two, He began to die.

These words mark the climax of the suffering of Christ for a lost world. His cry in Aramaic, "My God, My God, why hast thou forsaken me," testifies that He experiences separation from God as the sinner's substitute. Here the sorrow, grief, and pain are at their worst. He is wounded for out transgressions and gives Himself a "ransom for many." Him who knew no sin, God makes "to be sin for us." He dies forsaken, that we might never be forsaken. Thus, we are redeemed by the sufferings of Christ.

The sufferings of Christ, uttered in His final words with a loud voice, "It is finished!" This cry signified the end of His sufferings and the completion of the work of redemption. The debt for our sin was paid in full and the plan of salvation established. Only then, does He offer a final prayer, "Father, into Thy hands I commend my spirit."

Now, I know I can go through my trials and tribulations. It is nothing like what Jesus Christ went through. However, two weeks later I went to a funeral, the Pastor of that church told me in front of everybody that I was not welcome in his pulpit. I was so hurt that he said it in front of all the people. That night, I dreamed that the Lord was telling me not to worry, "The battle is not yours, its mine." Then I thought, be not forgetful to entertain strangers: for thereby some have entertained angels unawares (Hebrews 13:2). Being a Baptist female preacher, I knew that I had to go through a lot; I had to stay on my knees.

"These things I have spoken unto you that in me ye might have peace. In the world, ye shall have tribulation: but be of good cheer; I have overcome the world." Jesus is letting me know when He was on earth, He went through tribulations and He overcame this world. Now, it was my time. I have got to go through trials and tribulations and one day I will overcome this world.

I have always wanted a big faith; I did not want to be like Martha. We see the faith of Martha in connection with the resurrection of her brother, Lazarus. We recall the story of Lazarus' resurrection and how

Martha's faith was initially limited. However, as Martha's belief in the power of Christ increased, her brother was resurrected.

Do not be satisfied with limited, fundamental faith only, when you can have unlimited faith that pleases God and reveals His glory. I always wanted a BIG faith. When I pray, I go on and thank God for my blessing. Through it all God kept me in His arms. When I was young, in high school, I loved to dance, I would win every dance contest, and I was good at it. Now that God call me to preach His word, through all my ups and downs, I am going to be good at it. I was good dancing for the Devil, now I will be good at serving God.

Jesus was in great anguish over his coming physical pain, separation from the Father, and death for the sins of the world. The divine course was set, but he, in his human nature, still struggled. Because of the anguish he experienced, he can relate to our suffering. His strength to obey came from his relationship with God the Father, who is also the source of strength.

My cup was so bitter, so many church doors was close in my face. I kept the faith I knew some way and some how God would bring me through. I did not understand while I had to go through so much but now I understand.

When you see evil schemes unfold, remember that they will not succeed forever. The power of evildoers is only temporary, and God's very presence would send them scattering in a moment. God, according to his plan and purpose, will intervene for his people and give the wicked the judgment they deserve. We should not be dismayed when we see the temporary advantage God's enemies have.

God's loving concern does not begin on the day we are born and conclude on the day we die. It reaches back to those days before we were born, and reaches ahead along the unending path of eternity. Our only sure help comes from God whose concern for us reaches beyond our earthly existence. How can anyone reject such love?

Troubles, like "many waters," can threaten to drown us. How often we wish God would quickly rescue us out of our troubles. Remember that God can either deliver us or help us remain steady as we go through troubles. Either way, his protection is best for us. When you feel as though you are drowning in troubles, ask God to help you, hold you steady, and protect you. In his care, you are never helpless.

Some people think that belief in God is a crutch for weak people who cannot make it on their own. God is indeed a buckler (shield) to protect us when we are too weak to face certain trials by ourselves, but he does not want us to remain weak. He strengthens, protects, and guides us in order to send us back into an evil world to fight for him. Then God continues to work with us, because the strongest person on earth is infinitely weaker then God and need his help. You remember David was not a coward; he was a mighty warrior who, with all his armies and weapons, knew that only God could ultimately protect and save him.

God doesn't promise to eliminate challenges; instead, he promises to give us strength to meet those challenges. If he gave us no rough roads to walk, no mountains to climb, and no battles to fight, we would not grow. He does not leave us alone with our challenges, however. Instead he stands beside us, teaches us, and strengthens us to face them.

Prayer can release our tensions in times of emotional stress. Trusting God to be our rock, our salvation, and defense changes our entire outlook on life. No longer are we held captive by hurtful treatment from others. We are released to follow an unchanging God.

The judgment of God is coming against the wicked. God will pour out his fury on his enemies, and they will be forced to drink it. God will have the last word. He will decide the final outcome, settling all matters that concern both the wicked and the goodly. The former will eventually experience his judgment; the latter will experience his faithful love. No matter how dark your day may be, make it your continual practice to acknowledge God's sovereignty over your world. Tell him regularly how grateful you are that he has the final word.

Nothing but truth is acceptable to God. When we pray, sing, speak, or serve, nothing closes the door of God's acceptance more than hypocrisy, lying, or pretense. God sees through us and refuses to listen. To be close to God be honest with him.

> *Hear now this, O foolish people, and without understanding; which have eyes, and see not; which have ears, and hear not [Jeremiah 5:21].*

Have you ever listened to someone talk, only to realize that you haven't heard a word that was said? Jeremiah told the people their eyes and ears did them no good because they refused to see or hear God's message. The people of Judah and Israel were foolishly deaf when God promised blessings for obedience and destruction for disobedience. When God speaks through his Word or his messengers, we harm ourselves if we fail to listen. God's message will never change us unless we listen to it.

We're all encouraged by a leader who stirs us to move ahead, someone who believes we can do the task he has given and who will be with us all the way. God is that kind of leader. He knows our future, and his plans for us are good and full of hope. As long as God, who knows the future, provides our agenda and goes with us as we fulfill his mission, we can have boundless hope. This does not mean we will be spared pain, suffering, or hardship, but that God will see us through to a glorious conclusion.

> *For thus saith the LORD of hosts; After the glory hath he sent me unto the nations which spoiled you: for he that toucheth you toucheth the apple of his eye [Zech. 2:8].*

Believers are precious to God; they are his very own children. Treating any believer unkindly is the same as treating God that way. As Jesus told his disciples, when we help others we are helping him; when we neglect them we are neglecting him. Be careful, therefore, how you treat fellow believers-that is the way you are treating God.

God stays close to us even in death. When someone we love is nearing death, we may become angry and feel abandoned. But believers are precious to God, and he carefully chooses the time when they are to be called into his presence. Let this truth provide comfort when you've lost a loved one. God notices and each life is valuable to him. In the end Jesus will judge all who have oppressed God's people. God promises to live among his people, and he says that many nations will come to know him.

When we are wronged, often our first reaction is to get even. Instead, Jesus said we should do good to those who wrong us! Our desire should not be to keep score, but to love and forgive. This is not natural-it is supernatural. Only God can give us the strength to love as He does. Instead of planning vengeance, pray for those who hurt you.

We are saved by faith, not works. But love for others and for God is the response of those whom God has forgiven. God's forgiveness is complete, and Jesus said that those who are forgiven much love is given. Because faith expresses itself through love, you can check your love for others as a way to monitor your faith.

When believers lose the motivation of love they become critical of others. We stop looking for good in them and see only their faults. Soon we lose our unity. Have you ever talked behind someone's back? Have you focused on others' shortcomings instead of their strengths? Remind yourself of Jesus' command to love others as we love ourselves. When you begin to feel critical of someone, make a list of that person's positive qualities. When problems need to be addressed, confront in love rather than gossip.

A new commandment I give unto you, that ye love one another; as I have loved you, that ye also love one another. By this shall all *men* know that ye are my disciples, if ye have love one to another [John 13:34-35].

To love others was not a new commandment, but to love others as much as Christ loved others was revolutionary. Now we are to love others based on Jesus' sacrificial love for us. Such love will not only bring unbelievers to Christ, it will also keep believers strong and united in a world hostile to God. Jesus was a living example of God's love, as we are to be living examples of Jesus' love.

Love is simply warm feelings; it is an attitude that reveals itself in action. How can we love others as Jesus loves us? By helping when it is not convenient, by giving when it hurt, by devoting energy to others' welfare rather than our own, by absorbing hurts from others without complaining or fighting back. This kind of loving is hard to do. That is why people notice when you do it and know you are empowered by a supernatural source.

Everyone believes love is important, but we usually think of it as a feeling. In reality, love is a choice and an action. God is the source of our love: He loved us enough to sacrifice His Son for us. Jesus is our example of what it means to love; everything he did in life and death was supremely loving. The Holy Spirit gives us the power to love; He lives in our heart and makes us more and more like Jesus. God's love always involves a choice and an action, and our love should be like His. How well do you display your love for God in the choices you make and the actions you take?

THE JUST SHALL LIVE BY FAITH

Commanded are we to pray, and God has promised to answer. I had to learn the requirements for answers to prayer. We are to abide in Him (Jesus), that is, to continue in Him. It means to remain in His perfect will at all costs. His words are to "abide in me"; they are to become a vital part of our lives. I am filled with and guided by His words. Someone might say "I pray but God does not answer all my prayers." God has several responses to prayer. (1) The answer is sometimes immediate. Peter walked on the water to go to Jesus, and as he began to sink, he prayed, "Lord save me!" The answer was immediate. (2) The answer is sometimes delayed. The delay is according to His will. The resurrection of Lazarus is a good example of delayed answer to prayer. Lazarus was sick. Mary and Martha sent for Jesus to come and heal him. However, Jesus delayed coming until Lazarus was dead and in the tomb for four days. Then He came and raised Lazarus from the dead. The answer was delayed but not denied. (3) The answer is sometimes "NO." When God answers with a "NO," He always accompanies the answer with peace and grace. (4) The answer is sometimes different from what we expect. You pray for perseverance and God sends tribulation—because "tribulation produces perseverance." God answers all our prayers—not according to our wishes, but according to His perfect will.

I thought at one time that He had left me. I prayed and prayed, and I did not know what to do any more. [*Let your conversation be without covetousness; and be content with such things as ye have: for he hath said, I will never leave thee, nor forsake thee.*] In this terrible trial of suffering, I maintained my faith in Christ Jesus. I was assured that Christ would guard the true gospel and His ministry. The just shall live his or her whole life by faith. We are saved by faith, we are kept by faith, and we live by faith. I know my faith shall be tried many times and in many ways, but faith always vindicates, because it is more than equal to any occasion. Faith knows how to wait on the Lord, and it is always victorious.

Faith says, "God is working out His perfect will in my life, and I can wait, endure, and suffer." Faith does not make anything easy, but it does make all things possible. I am so glad that God blessed me with a good husband. He has been with me from the first day that I told him that God called me to preach. He told me that he would not stand in my way because he did not know what God told me.

My husband has been a great husband. He has submitted himself to God and to me. [*Submitting yourselves one to another in the fear of God. Ephesians 5:21*] Submission to one another in Christ is a general spiritual principle. This principle is applied first to the Christian family. Submission, humility, gentleness, patience, and forbearance must be characteristic of each member of the family. The wife must submit to the husband's responsibility of leadership of the family. The husband must submit to the needs of the wife in an attitude of love and self-giving.

At the church that I joined with my husband, my Pastor and his wife took me in just as though I were one of their children. I began doing Women Day Programs for other churches. I was also given chances to preach at my Church. After years of working together, my Pastor had a stroke. He decided to let go of the Church. The same Sunday that he told the members that he was resigning, the Church voted me in. I could not believe it! Me! A Pastor of a Church! **A Baptist Church**! I became the first female Baptist Pastor in the county. I remember my Pastor was out of town. I took over for him at our Church and that evening we went to another church. The Pastor there told me that he had made a covenant with his Deacons when he took the church not to let women come into his pulpit. I thought, "You own nothing in this world. You will carry nothing out of this world."

Jesus answered and said unto them, Verily I say unto you, If ye have faith, and doubt not ye shall not only do this which is done to the fig tree, but also if ye shall say unto this mountain, Be thou removed, and be thou cast into the sea; it shall be done (Matt. 21:21).

Many have wondered about Jesus' statement that if we have faith and don't doubt, we can move mountains. Jesus, of course, was not suggesting that his followers use prayer as "magic" and perform capricious mountain-moving acts. Instead, he was making a strong point about the disciples and our lack of faith. What kinds of mountains do you face? Have you talked to God about them? How strong is your faith?

Why did Jesus curse the fig tree? This was not a thoughtless, angry act, but an acted-out parable. Jesus was showing his anger at religion without substance. Just as the fig tree looked good from a distance but was fruitless at close examination, so the Temple looked impressive at first glance, but its sacrifices and other activities were hollow because they were not done to worship God sincerely. If you only appear to have faith without putting it to work in your life, you are like the fig tree that withered and died because it bore no fruit. Genuine faith means bearing fruit for God's Kingdom.

And he said unto them, "Why are ye so fearful? How is it that ye have no faith" (Mark 4:40)? Problems occur in every area of life. The disciples needed rest, but they encountered a terrible storm. The Christian life may have more stormy weather than calm seas. As Christ's follower, be prepared for the storms that will surely come. Do not surrender to the stress, but remain resilient and recover from setbacks. With faith in Christ, you can pray, trust, and move ahead. When a squall approaches, lean into the wind and trust God.

The disciples lived with Jesus, but they underestimated Him. They did not see that His power applied to their own situation. Jesus has been with His people for 20 centuries, and yet we, like the disciples, underestimate His power to handle crises in our lives. The disciples did not yet know enough about Jesus. We cannot make the same excuse.

Just as a fruit tree is expected to bear fruit, God's people should produce a crop of good deeds. God has no use for those who call themselves Christians but live otherwise. Like many people in John's day who were God's people in name only, we are of no value to God if we are Christians in name only. If others cannot see our faith in the way we treat them, we may not be God's people at all. We often assume that Jesus' disciples were great men of faith from the time they met Jesus. But they had to grow in their faith just as all believers do. This is apparently not the only time Jesus called Peter, James, and John to follow Him. Although it took time for Jesus' call and his message to get through, the disciples followed. In the same way, we may question and falter, but we must never stop following Jesus.

> *And, behold, men brought in a bed a man which was taken with a palsy: and they sought to lay him before him. And when they could not find by what way means to bring him in, and they might bring him in because of the multitude, they went upon the housetop, and let him down through the tiling with his couch into the midst before Jesus [Luke 5:18-19].*

It was not the sick man's faith that impressed Jesus, but the faith of his friends. Jesus responded to their faith and healed the man. For better or worse, our faith attracts others. We cannot make another person a Christian, but we can do much through our words, actions, and love to give him or her a chance to respond. Look for opportunities to bring your friends to the living Christ.

The disciples had been unable to cast out this devil, and they asked Jesus why. He pointed to their lack of faith. It is the power of God, plus our faith, that moves mountains. The mustard seed was the smallest particle imaginable. Jesus said that even faith as small or undeveloped as a mustard seed would have been sufficient. Perhaps they had tried to cast out the devil with their own ability rather than God's. There is great potential in even a little faith when we trust in God's power to act. If we feel weak or powerless as Christians, we should examine our faith, making sure we are trusting God's power, not our own abilities to produce results. Jesus was not condemning the disciples for substandard faith; he was trying to show how important faith would be in their future ministry. If you are facing a problem that seems as big and immovable as a mountain, turn your eyes from the mountain and look to Jesus for more faith. Only then will you be able to overcome the obstacles that stand in your way.

> *And when Jesus departed thence, two blind men followed him, crying, and saying, Thou son of David, have mercy on us. And when he was come into the house, the blind men came to him: and Jesus saith unto them, Believe ye that I am able to do this? They said unto him, Yea, Lord* [Matt. 10:27-28].

Jesus did not respond immediately to the blind men's pleas. He waited to see if they had faith. Not everyone who says he or she wants help really believes God can help them. Jesus may have waited and questioned these men to emphasize and increase their faith. If it seems that God is too slow in answering your prayers, maybe he is testing you as he did the blind men. Do you believe God can help you?

"Thou son of David" was a popular way of addressing Jesus as the Messiah, because it was known that the Messiah would be a descendant of David. This is the first time the title is used in Matthew. Jesus' ability to heal the blind was prophesied in Isaiah 29:18; 35:5;42:7. These blind men were persistent. They went right into the house where Jesus was staying. They knew Jesus could heal them, and they would let nothing stop them from finding him. That is faith. If you believe Jesus is the answer to your every need, don't let anything or anyone stop you from reaching him.

Jesus told the people to keep quiet about his healings because he did not want to be known only as a miracle worker. He healed because he had compassion on people, but he also wanted to bring *spiritual* healing to a sin-sick world.

Jesus' words do not mean we can automatically obtain anything we want if we just think positively. Jesus meant that anything is possible if we believe because nothing is too difficult for God. We cannot have everything we pray for as if by magic; but with faith, we can have everything we need to serve him. The attitude of trust and confidence that the Bible calls *belief or faith* is not something we can obtain without help. Faith is a gift from God. No matter how much faith we have, we never reach the point of being self-sufficient. Faith is not stored away like money in the bank. Growing in faith is a constant process of daily renewing our trust in Jesus.

The disciples would often face difficult situations that could be resolved only through prayer. Prayer is the key that unlocks faith in our lives. Effective prayer needs both the attitude of complete dependence and the action of asking. Prayer demonstrates our reliance on God as we humbly invite God to fill us with faith and power. There is no substitute for prayer, especially in circumstances that seem impossible.

To feel secure, all children need is a loving look and gentle touch from someone who cares. They believe us because they trust us. Jesus said that people should believe in him with this kind of childlike faith. We do not have to understand all the mysteries of the universe; it should be enough to know that God loves us and provides forgiveness for our sin.

Why does God save us by faith alone? (1) Faith eliminates the pride of human effort, because faith is not a deed that we do. (2) Faith exalts what God has done, not what people do. (3) Faith admits that we can not keep the Law or measure up to God's standards-we need help. (4) Faith is based on our relationship with God, not our performance for God.

The disciples' request was genuine; they wanted the faith necessary for such radical forgiveness. But Jesus did not directly answer their question, because the amount of faith is not as important as its genuineness. What is faith? It is total dependence on God and a willingness to do his will. It is not something we use to put on a show for others. It is complete and humble obedience to God's will, readiness to do whatever he calls us to do. The amount of faith is not as important as the right King of faith-faith in our all-powerful God. A mustard seed is small, but it is alive and growing. Like a tiny seed, a small amount of genuine faith in God will take root and grow. Almost invisible at first, the seed will begin to spread, first underground and then visibly. Although each change will be gradual and imperceptible, soon this faith will have produced major results that will uproot and destroy competing loyalties. We do not need more faith; a tiny seed of faith is enough, if it is alive and growing.

The Valley Of The Shadow Of Death

My mother had suffered a stroke four years prior. She was growing weak. But, in April 2008, as I took over the church and was ordained, my mother was there. We had to bring her in a wheelchair; she would not have missed it for the world! My mother was growing weaker and weaker. She was my mother, my friend; we lived side by side. I stayed at her house as much as I stayed at mine. She began to go in and out of the hospital. She had gotten to the point when she came home, I would have to stay with her. One Saturday, as I was giving her a bath, I could not stand her up. It was just as if she did not know who I was. I knew instantly she was in deep trouble. My heart was racing. It was about three in the evening and I called my other sister and brothers. I knew that she had another stroke. I called 911. My heart was in my throat. She stayed in the hospital for five days. When I went to pick her up, she could not walk at all. All this happened in August 2008.

Just as I had gotten the church, everything was going fine. She stayed in her home and we just moved in with her. Later on, my baby sister and her family moved in with Mama. She was getting weaker day by day. Mama had to go back to the hospital. Her doctor sent her to rehabilitation. She stayed for two weeks without getting any better. She had stopped eating, she was just like a baby. I prayed and I prayed, but God did not answer my prayer the way I wanted Him to. I found out there are some prayers He does not answer. I thought, "God have you left us?" Her body was as limp as a dishrag. She had lost all control of her bodily functions. The nurses and doctors had poked her everywhere she could be poked. She was not getting any better, and we knew it. Before she got so weak, she had called me one day and said to me, "Baby, I want you to preach the Word, do not let anyone stop you. I want you to keep praying and keep the faith. Keep preaching. Do not stop God's work for anything." I remembered her words of encouragement, so I kept preaching, praying and kept the faith. I had never walked through such a deep valley as the valley of the shadow of death before.

I had never thought about Mama getting sick; never thought about her leaving us. One night, the nurse called from rehab and told us that they were sending her back to the hospital. Her stool was all blood! My sisters and I met them at the hospital. Her body was so weak; she never knew that we were there. I was so weak in my body; I thought I just could not take it. I thought, "God where are you?" In addition, on that Sunday I had to go in those doors at church, smile at the people, and preach. It was not fair. However, is life fair? They put mama back in ICU. My brothers and sisters and I took turns working through family crises. I continued to teach, preach, and encourage others. Every now and then, when no one was around, I sat and washed my face of tears. My heart was cracked, and inside, I thought I was coming apart.

I had my job. Everyday, I would witness, telling people how to pray, how to have faith, how to be patient, how to stand still and let the Lord fight your battle. That was a lot to maintain because, at the same time, I had to hide my own pain. The sixth day they moved my Mama to a room out of ICU and the doctor met us in the room. Mama was like in a deep sleep. The doctor told us that her body was shutting down. I asked, "What do you mean?" Her liver had stopped functioning and the rest of her body was shutting down so it was just a matter of time. I got so upset! I thought, "It is not over until God say it is over!" I thought, "Lord, help us through this crisis!" Again, I thought, "God where are you?" When I went to bed that night, I dreamed that God told me, "I am with you. I am carrying you." She was the one in a deep sleep. But, it was as if I were having a bad dream. However, this time it was no dream for either of us. I kept thinking, "There is nothing too hard for God." I thought it would get better, but it did not.

The hospital sent her to a rest home about two blocks from her home so we could see about her. She did not know where she was. I thought I would die. Our father died in 1995, he had suffered for eight years. I was strong, then. I had preached his funeral. It was different with Mama. She would always ask me, "Baby, when I am gone to be with the Lord, will you preach my funeral?" I thought that I could, but I could not. She was all we had left. I thought I would lose my mind and faint, but I continued to preach on Sunday, lead Bible study on Wednesday night, and keep a smile. The Church did not know the pain I had in my heart. As I stood there watching her slowly leave us, everyone had tears in their eyes. I kept praying, "Lord, help me to be strong." I needed strength to accept the things I could not change. The scriptures came alive in my pain. I knew what to do when pain will not stop. I finally realized that not every story has a happy ending; at least not the one we were going through. My mother was lying there dying and I could not do anything about it. God was in full control, and I knew it. I knew that God would not put any more on me than I could bare. Just sitting there, waiting on the last breath, "Lord, help me!" I never knew that her life would have this huge detour toward the end of her journey.

My brothers, sisters, and I watched a hard working woman slowly slip away. My mother and father raised seven children, three girls and four boys. They raised us up, teaching us about Jesus Christ. They taught us how to pray and have faith, taught us how to love people, and how to work for what we wanted. They sent us to school and took us to church. Now, she lay struggling for every breath. I prayed and prayed. I had seen God heal. Why not my own mother? I spoke the Word! I stood on His promise! And finally, as I sobbed on the pillow, I prayed the prayer of faith. It hurt so bad, my heart ached. We become powerless. I learned some things about God's silence. I had spent much time learning His Word, but I never thought about God's silence. Whenever He does not speak a word, He is teaching in the stillness.

Patience is what God gives you when bad things remain unchanged. Patience is what He teaches in His silence. Faith comes by hearing, but patience comes only by absolute silence. *[And not only so, but we glory in tribulations also: knowing that tribulation worketh patience. Romans 5:3]* Paul lists "tribulations" as one of the blessings of our salvation in Christ. God's grace enables us to look beyond our present problems to a fervent hope in God and a certain hope for the return of our Lord to establish righteousness and godliness in the new heaven and earth. In the meantime, while on this earth, we have the love of God shed abroad in our hearts by the Holy Spirit in order to comfort us in our trials and bring Christ's presence. If the trial is going to be a long one, we all must learn to run with patience.

I stood there and saw my mother just slip away from us. She is gone to never come back to us, not on this earth. She was gone. I could not imagine my life without her, but the tribulations of her extended illness have been a genuine gift from God through the love she and I shared. Caring for her, loving her, suffering with her, through the transition from life unto death is part of our existence.

Is God still good? Of course, He is. I have learned that He is there in the race with you, coaching you, teaching you, and sometimes, even carrying you. He allows my soul to be stretched like everyone else's. It is just that He uses different things with different people. It is there at the point of strain that we find patience and a clearer view of God's grace.

My mother worked so hard for her children. She had taught us how to live, and now she taught us how to die. I can still hear her final breath. She had reached her final destination, and all I could say was, "Farewell, Mama. I'll meet you on the other side. I'll see you in the morning."

I knew the Word. I had lived, day-by-day, the Word of God, but the hurt was so bad, I could not let go. I made myself sick, but, I still preached on Sunday and held Bible study. I still smiled, even when I did not feel like it. I lost 45 lb. I felt like I was in another world. I knew I had to let go and let God. We must try to see God at work in whatever trials come our way. We must remember that God's expectations are bigger than our own. When my mother passed away, everyone offered me kind remarks about her new home in Heaven. I know that they were trying to comfort me. Comfort comes in its own good time, and that is okay, because sometimes we need to allow time for the heart to heal.

My torn ligaments, my heartbreaks, my soul aches are all part of the process. Through Mama's passing, I became a much stronger person. As the old Gospel song declares, "I come this far by faith, leaning on Jesus." Grief will come and go, but you must persevere gradually. What ever you do, do not drown in your own pool of grief. I was so tired; I felt that we had run a race. Now, I am loose enough to run with patience the course that God has set for me to run. You learn that when trouble persists long enough, you begin to accept what you cannot change.

The lesson I learned is that we must see these trials as opportunities to fulfill God's work. It may seem like we are working our own way through these trials, but the truth is that we are glorifying our God and becoming more like the perfect example of His Son.

We must remember that only our Father and His purposes, no matter how painful they may seem now, truly satisfy our souls. Even the things that I thought would kill me only stretched me until I developed the limber, relaxed posture of a patient woman who walks, runs and occasionally, crawls with God. God tells us that we are to run with patience.

[But those who wait on the Lord shall renew their strength; they shall mount up with wings like eagles, they shall run and not be weary, they shall walk and not faint. Isaiah 40:31] I like the way the Prophet Isaiah said this, "Those times when we feel like we are too tired to run, walk, or even crawl, He carries us and sustains us. He gives us wings of faith on which to fly. He becomes the wind beneath our wings."

We do our part and our Lord does His. However silent He may seem in the moment, sometimes, you just have to steady your pace and face your life. You cannot fix everything. Calm yourself, steady your course, relinquish your fears, do not dwell on the past or worry about the future. Just lift your head up, keep your back straight, and run with patience the race that is set before you. Feel the wind of Jesus' breath beneath your wings and soar beyond your own expectations!

How do you argue with Almighty God? Do you demand answers when things do not go your way? You lose a job? Someone close to you is ill or dies? Finances are tight? You fail? Or unexpected changes occur? The next time you are tempted to complain to God, consider how much He loves you.

Many people think that believing in God protects them from trouble, so when calamity comes, they question God's goodness and justice. But my message to you is to not give up on God just because bad things happen. Faith in God does not guarantee personal prosperity, and lack of faith does not guarantee troubles in this life. If this were so, people would believe in God simply to get rich. God is capable of rescuing us from suffering, but he may also allow suffering to come for reasons we cannot understand. It is Satan's strategy to get us to doubt God at exactly this moment. If we always know why we suffer, our faith will have no room to grow.

Paul reminds us that a victorious life in the spirit is no easy path. Jesus suffered, and we who follow Him will suffer. Consider suffering as suffering with Him.

God has opened doors for me that I thought would never open. Jesus told me in Revelation 3:8, I know thy works: behold, I have set before thee an open door, and no man can shut it: for thou hast a little strength, and hast kept my word, and hast not denied my name.

There were three occasions on which women displayed their love for Jesus by anointing him with precious perfumes. This woman is unnamed, but her act is memorialized. She anointed Jesus just two days before His crucifixion. Unlike the other anointing women, she poured it on Christ's head rather than His feet. Again, there were objections. [*"Wouldn't it have been better to sell the ointment and give the money to the poor?" Jesus responded, "Why do you trouble the woman, for she has done a good work for me. For you have the poor with you always, but me you do not have always. For in pouring this fragrant oil on my body, she did it for my burial. Assuredly, I say to you, wherever this gospel is preached in the whole world, what this woman has done will also be told as a memorial to her" Matt. 26:10-13*].

Jesus' words bring the woman's action into focus. He said, "She did it for my burial." We do not know whether the woman understood the significance of her action, but Matthew 26:1 tells us that Jesus had just told "His disciples" that He was about to be crucified. Since women were among His disciples, it is possible that she knew what she was doing. Hers was undoubtedly an act of love, but it may well have signaled an understanding of what Jesus faced that the male disciples lacked.

This anointing, and that of the other anointing women, was destined to be the only anointing Jesus' body would receive. Before the women who planned to anoint his body returned to the tomb where Jesus laid, He had risen from the dead.

There is no wonder that the retelling of this incident is a "memorial to her." It was this woman and, quite possibly, Mary of Bethany who alone were sensitive to the suffering Jesus would soon face. In anointing him, the anointing women showed that they shared his pain.

I pray about the things that would normally worry me. I refuse to spend my time worrying about things over which I have no control, everybody, everything is in God's hands. [*I have set the LORD always before me: because he is at my right hand, I shall not be moved. Psalms 16:8*]. This teaches us that believers should seek and cherish above all else an intimate fellowship with God. The Lord's continual presence at our right hand brings His guidance, protection, resurrection, and eternal blessings. I believe everything has a season, a time for every purpose under heaven (Eccles. 3:1). I had to learn that I could not change how some people felt about me becoming a preacher. Some people would laugh at me; some people would send me notes telling me that I was disobeying God's Word that a woman is not to be the head of man. People would call me on the phone and hang up.

Then the Spirit once again lead me to the Scripture: *There is neither Jew nor Greek, there is neither bond nor free, there is neither male nor female: for ye are all one in Christ Jesus (Gal. 3:28)*. Paul removes all ethnic, racial, national, social, and sexual distinctions with regard to one's spiritual relationship with Jesus Christ. All in Christ are equal heirs of the grace of life, the promised Spirit, and renewal in the image of God. On the other hand, within the context of spiritual equality, men remain men and women remain women. Their God-assigned roles in marriage and society remain unchanged.

[*Likewise, ye husbands, dwell with them according to knowledge, giving honour unto the wife, as unto the weaker vessel, and as being heirs together of the grace of life; that your prayers be not hindered. 1 Peter 3:7*]. Then, I asked, "What is Peter saying?" He mentions three things that husbands must be concerned about with regard to their wives. (1) They must be considerate and understanding, living with their wives in love and harmony with God's Word. (2) They must show respect to them as equal heirs of the grace of God and salvation. This requires that wives be honored, provided for, helped, and protected according to their needs. "Weaker" probably refers to the woman's physical strength. A husband must praise and highly treasure his wife as she endeavors to love and help him according to God's will. (3) They must be concerned about unjust and improper treatment of their wives. Peter indicates that a husband who fails to live with his wife in an understanding way and to give her honor as a fellow child of God will damage his relation with God by creating a barrier between his prayers and God.

I knew what God had called me to do. I just humbled myself under the mighty hand of God, that he may exalt me in due time. Jesus taught his disciples that unless you become as a little child, you will not inherit the kingdom. I had to learn to pray for all the people that talked about me: the ones who closed the church doors in my face.

Blessed are the pure in heart: for they shall see God. The "pure in heart" are those who have been delivered from the power of sin by the grace of God and now strive without deceit to please and glorify God and to be like Him. Only the pure in heart "shall see God." To see God means to be His child and dwell in His presence, both now and in the future kingdom.

Blessed are they which are persecuted for righteousness sake, for theirs is the kingdom of heaven (Matt. 5:8-10). Grace is God's presence, favor, and power. It is a force, a heavenly strength bestowed on those who call upon God. This grace will descend upon the faithful believer who accepts his weaknesses and difficulties for the gospel's sake. The greater our weakness and trials for Christ, the more grace God will give us to accomplish His will. What he bestows on us is always sufficient for us to live our daily lives, to work for Him, and to endure our suffering and "thorns in the flesh." As long as we draw near to Christ, Christ will bestow His heavenly strength and comfort on us.

My journey has been filled with a lot of trials and tribulations. God can and He will work things out for His glory. I learned that I had to let go and let God do His work. It was time for me to be still. He tells us in His Word to "... *be still, and know that I am God: I will be exalted among the heathen, I will be exalted in the earth (Psalms 46:10)*.

The Hebrew meaning here for "*be still*" can also be translated "*let go*", quit holding on to things that keep you from exalting God and giving Him His proper places in your life.

When we face baffling affliction, a human response is to feel sorry for ourselves. Our pain lures us toward self-pity. At this point, we are only one step from self-righteousness, where we keep track of life's injustices and say, "Look what happened to me! How unfair it is!" We may feel like blaming God. Remember that life's trials, whether allowed by God or sent by God, is the means for development and refinement. When facing trials, ask, "What can I learn and how can I grow?' rather than "who did this to me and how can I get rid of it?'

LET GOD BE THE JUDGE

For three years I dreamed that God was telling me to go preach His Word. I did not want to think about the dream because I knew how so many people felt about women preachers. After three years I got tired and said, "Lord, here I am." In my dream, God instructed me what to preach in a sermon about what to say. God called me to preach His Word, and for a subject: LET GOD BE THE JUDGE. So many people were judging me. God wanted them to know that He is the judge; we judge no one. I did not know that I had to go through such a deep valley, to tell people about Jesus Christ, to repent for their sins. [A*nd if thou shalt confess with thy mouth the Lord Jesus, and shalt believe in thine heart that God hath raised him from the dead, thou shalt be saved.*] So many times people tried to beat me down, but this time when I was so down, I thought about what Jesus said, "My grace is sufficient for thee: for my strength is made perfect in weakness.

 A judge is an official authorized to hear and decide cases of law. The judge has the final say and the last words. Jesus said in John 8:15, "You judge according to the flesh, I judge no one; and if I do judge, my judgment is true for I am not alone, but I am with the Father who sent me. Judge not and you shall not be judged. Condemn not and you shall not be condemned. Forgive, and you will be forgiven.

 I have learned in my walk with Christ discouragement will come, especially to a preacher and teacher's life. Sometime the heartaches are real, especially when you are misunderstood and when your motives are judged harshly. I learned to look up and say, "God You Are My Judge!"

When mama and daddy took us to church on communion Sunday, I had to do communion the next week with my brothers and sister. If we went to a funeral, I would do the funeral. I wonder if that was part of God teaching me. After hearing a sermon on Sunday, the next week I would preach that same sermon.

Through my journey, I learned to be silent because a faithful believer may, at times, feel that God is not listening to his or her prayers. This experience, however, will not be the norm as long as we continue to draw near to God through Christ. After a period of trials, the Lord will respond and help us as a shepherd cares for his sheep.

[*O LORD, my God, in thee do I put my trust: save me from all them that persecute me, and deliver me. Psalms 7:1*]. In reading this Psalms, those who have sincerely committed themselves to God may with all confidence take refuge in the Lord and commit their life situations to Him. In the midst of unjust or troublesome times, we may place ourselves under the protection of God and appeal to Him based on our faithfulness and righteousness.

God created us for His glorious purpose. We are not just animals, the product of natural evolution or chance. We are so valuable to God that we are special objects of His concern and favor. He has honored us by choosing us to rule over His creation. So many times, like Jesus Himself, we feel forsaken by God. When this occurs, hold fast to your belief in God and in His goodness, and continue to pray and trust in Him.

[*My GOD, my God, why hast thou forsaken me? Why art thou so far from helping me, and from the words of my roaring? Psalm 22:1*] I would wake late in the night and pray, as I said earlier. I thought people would want to hear the word of God regardless of who was preaching it, a man or woman. How wrong I was.

[*And it shall come to pass afterward, that I will pour out my spirit upon all flesh; and your sons and your daughters shall prophesy, your old men shall dream dreams, your young men shall see visions. Joel 2:28*]. Joel predicts a day when God would pour out His Spirit on all those who "call on the name of the LORD." This outpouring will result in a charismatic flow of the Spirit of prophecy among God's people. This prophecy is an ongoing promise to all who accept Christ as Lord, for all believers can and should be filled with the Holy Spirit. I never thought that I would go through so much suffering, when the only thing I was doing was telling men and women, boys and girls that Jesus loves them. [*That if thou shalt confess with thy mouth the Lord Jesus, and shalt believe in thine heart that God hath raised Him from the dead, thou shalt be saved. Romans 10:9*].

Is it so wrong for a woman to preach God's Word? God used Mary Magdalene to carry the first sermon after Jesus was raised from the dead. [*Then said Jesus unto them, "Be not afraid: go tell my brethren that they go into Galilee, and there shall they see me." Matt. 28:10*]. Why were these women not to be afraid? The angel's response gives us the answer: "for I know that ye seek Jesus." The women had remained loyal friends of Jesus when the world despised and crucified Him. At Christ's return for His faithful, they will have no reason to fear if they also have remained loyal to Him in the midst of a world that rejects His love, salvation, and holy Word.

Every now and then, He does us a favor. Yes, favor is something we did not earn or can only explain as the loving hand of God. He knows when the load is overwhelming. Many times, He moves just in the knick of time.

The spirit of the Lord told me one night in a dream, "I am with you." This promise is Christ's assurance to those involved in winning the lost and teaching them to observe His righteous standards. Jesus arose, is now alive, and is personally interested in each one of His children. He is with us in the person of the Holy Spirit and through His Word. No matter what your condition is—weak, poor, humble, and apparently unimportant—He cares for you, watches with concern every detail of life's trials and struggles, and gives both the grace that is sufficient and His presence to guide you home. This is the Christian's answer to every fear, every doubt, every trouble, heartache, and discouragement.

I thought at one time that I could please men, but I remember what my mother told me one day we were talking. She said, "You will never please man. You try to please God and everything will fall in place." She told me to go to Galatians 1:10, where it says, "For do I now persuade men, or God? Or do I seek to please men? For if I yet pleased men, I should not be the servant of Christ." And I thought," Paul, what are you talking about?"

For if I yet pleased men. One cannot be a genuine minister of the Gospel and attempt to please people by compromising the truths of the Gospel. Paul regarded it his duty to speak "not as pleasing men, but God, "who trieth our hearts." All believers of the Gospel of Christ must make it their aim, as did Paul, to please God, even if it means displeasing some people.

God is the only One Who has the right to condemn or sentence, therefore, when we pass judgment on another, we are, in a certain sense, setting ourselves up as God in that person's life. Each of us belong to God, and even though we have weaknesses, He is able to make us stand and to justify us. We answer to God, not to each other; therefore, we are not to judge one another in a critical way.

At the end of the world, angels will separate the evil from the good. There are true and false believers in churches today, but we should be cautious in our judgments because only Christ is qualified to make the final separation. If you start judging, you may damage some of the good "plants." It's more important to judge your own response to God than to analyze others' responses.

Jesus Christ has been given the authority to judge all the earth. Although his judgment is already working in our lives, there is a future, final judgment when Christ returns and everyone's life will be reviewed and evaluated. This will not be confined to nonbelievers. Christians, too, will face judgment. Their eternal destiny is secure, but Jesus will look at how they handled gifts, opportunities, and responsibilities in order to determine their heavenly rewards. At the time of judgment, God will deliver the righteous and condemn the wicked. We should not judge others' salvation; that is God's work.

It is tempting to judge a fellow Christian, evaluating whether or not he or she is a good follower of Christ. But only God knows a person's heart, and he is the only one with the right to judge. Paul's warning to the Corinthians should also warn us. We are to confront those who are sinning, but we must not judge who is a better servant for Christ. When you judge someone, you invariably consider yourself better, and this is pride. People were judging me without knowing what God was doing in my life. We must be careful to avoid making judgments about a person, because God may be working in ways we know nothing about. After receiving much criticism, I was still able to pray for my friends. It is difficult to forgive someone who has accused you of wrong doing, but I did. Are you praying for those who have wronged you?

But ye are forgers of lies; ye are all physicians of no value (Job 13:4). Job compared his three friends to doctors who did not know what they were doing. They were like eye surgeons trying to perform open-heart surgery. Many of their ideas about God were true, but they did not apply to Job's situation. They were right to say that God is just. They were right to say God punishes sin. But they were wrong to assume that Job's suffering was a just punishment for his sin. They took a true principle and applied it wrongly, ignoring the vast differences in human circumstances. We must be careful and compassionate in how we apply biblical condemnations to the lives of others; we must be slow to judge others. If God were to answer all our questions, we would not be adequately tested. What if God had said, "Job, Satan's going to test you and afflict you, but in the end you'll be healed and get everything back?" Job's greatest test was not the pain and suffering, but that he did not know why it happened. Our greatest test may be that we must trust God's goodness even though we don't understand why our lives are going in a certain direction. We must learn to trust in the God who is good and not in the goodness of life.

I found out, through my trials, the secret of a close relationship with God is to pray to Him earnestly in the morning. In the morning, our minds are freer from problems and then we can commit the whole day to God. Regular communication helps any friendship and is certainly necessary for a strong relationship with God. We need to communicate with Him daily. Do you have a regular time to pray and read God's Word? Have you ever been falsely accused or badly hurt and wanted revenge? Instead of taking matters into your own hands and striking back, cry out to God for justice. The proper response to slander is prayer, not revenge, because God says, "Vengeance is mine; I will repay." Instead of striking back, ask God to take your case, bring justice, and restore your reputation.

God will never forsake those who trust in him. To forsake someone is to abandon that person. God's promise does not mean that if we trust in him we will escape loss of suffering; it means that God himself will never leave us no matter what we face.

All of us want God to help us when we are in trouble, but often for different reasons. Some want God's help so that they will be successful and other people will like them. Others want God's help so that they will be comfortable and feel good about themselves. When you call to God for help, consider your motive. Is it to save you pain and embarrassment or to bring God glory and honor?

So many times going through my trials, God seemed so far away. I did not stop praying or assume that God no longer cared. I was not complaining, but simply asking God to hurry to my aid. It is during those times, when we feel most alone or oppressed, that we need to keep praying, keep telling God about our troubles.

Can we expect God to care for us so others won't scoff at our beliefs? In the end, God's glory will be evident to all people, but in the meantime, we must endure suffering with patience and allow God to purify us through it. For reasons we do not know. We should be prepared for criticism, jokes, and unkind remarks because God does not place us beyond the attacks of scoffers.

Sometimes our trouble or pain is so great that all we can do is cry out to God, "Preserve my soul" or "Protect me." We feel so poor and needy. Many times when there is no relief in sight, all we can do is acknowledge the greatness of God and wait for better days ahead.

We should turn from sin because Christ is coming to judge the earth; we should be fervent in our service because we have little time before he returns. We should be prepared for Jesus to return because we don't know when he will come.

So many times when things go wrong, we tend to blame others for our miseries. Blaming others is easier than owning our share of the responsibility, but it is both destructive and sinful. Before you judge others for their shortcomings, remember that Christ the judge will come to evaluate each of us. He will not let us get away with shifting the blame to others.

All believers, we are "strangers and pilgrims" in this world because our real home is with God. Heaven is not the pink-cloud-and-harp existence popular in cartoons. Heaven is where God dwells. It operates to God's principles and values, and it is eternal and unshakable.

Someday, after God judges and destroys all sin, the Kingdom of heaven will rule every corner of this earth. John saw this day in a vision, and he cried out, "Behold, the tabernacle of God is with men, and he will dwell with them, and they shall be his people, and God himself shall be with them, and be their God"

Our real home, our true loyalty, should not be to this earth because it will be destroyed. Our loyalty should be to God's truth, his way of life, and his dedicated people. Because of this, we often feel like strangers in a world that would prefer to ignore God. All who follow Jesus must be prepared to suffer. Our goal should be to face suffering as he did-with patience, calmness, and confidence that God is in control of the future.

In order to accept Christ as Savior, we need to turn from our sins and willingly nail our sinful nature to the cross. This doesn't mean, however, that we will never see traces of our evil desires again. As Christians we still have the capacity to sin, but we have been set free from sin's power over us and no longer have to give in to it. We must daily commit our sinful tendencies to God's control, daily crucify them, and moment by moment draw on the Spirit's power to overcome them.

God is interested in every part of our life, not just the spiritual part. As we live by the Holy Spirit's power we need to submit every aspect of our life to God-emotional, physical, social, intellectual, vocational. Paul says, in essence, "You're saved, so live like it!" The Holy Spirit is the source of your new life, so walk with him. Don't let anything or anyone else determine your values and standards in any area of your life.

We all need a certain amount of approval from others. But those who go out of their way to secure honors or to win popularity become conceited and show that they are not following the Holy Spirit's leading. Those who look to God for approval won't need to envy others. As God's sons and daughters, we have his Holy Spirit as the loving guarantee on his approval. Seek to please God, and the approval of others won't seem so important.

No one should ever think he or she is totally independent and doesn't need help from others, and no one should feel excused from the task of helping others. The body of Christ the universal church-functions only when the members work together for the common good. Is there someone near you who needs help in a task of daily living? Is there a Christian brother or sister who needs correction or encouragement? Humbly and gently reach out to that person and offer to lift his or her load.

When you do your very best, you feel good about the results, and there is no need to compare yourself with others. People make comparisons for many reasons. Some point out others' flaws in order to feel better about them. Others simply want reassurance that they are doing well. When you are tempted to compare, look at Jesus Christ. His example will inspire you to do your very best, and his loving acceptance will comfort you when you fall short of your goals.

THE RAPTURE

I have always been a dreamer; God sometimes reveals His will to us through prophetic dreams. Although His primary revelation and guidance comes through Scripture, and the indwelling Holy Spirit, the Spirit of the Lord showed to me, in a dream, His returning for His church. In my dream, this angel took me to a grave yard and said to me, "Look." As I looked, the graves started breaking open. I saw people ascending to heaven. I saw little children and babies, going up to be with the Lord. There were so many graves left. I thought, "My God! What's happening?" In my dream I was walking down the road with this angel, he told me to look in front of me there were three women walking. Suddenly, the woman in the middle was gone. The angel said, "Come on, follow me." He took me to a house. There was a woman swinging her baby. The angel said to me, "Watch." In a moment, in the twinkling of an eye, the baby was gone! The mother was screaming and crying looking for her baby. The baby was gone to be with the Lord. At that point, I wanted to wake up out of that dream, but I could not.

The angel said, "One more place I want you to see." He took me to a big church. Again he said, "Follow me." We went in the back of the church, through a side door. The angel said, "I want you to see everything that is going to happen." The church was full of people. In the pulpit were seven preachers. The choir stand was full, they were singing, and praying. It sounded so good. However, this angel said to me, "Watch." People all over the church were being caught up together to meet the Lord in the air. I looked in the pulpit. Preachers were being caught up. In the choir stand, choir members were being caught up. Everybody was crying and screaming because they did not know what was going on. The angel said to me, "Look at all these people left." More people were left than the Lord took up.

The rapture had taken place! More people in the church were left than went to meet Jesus! Jesus came and got His Church, and so many were not ready. When I woke up, I was so afraid! My heart was beating rapidly!

> *[1 Thes. 4:16-17 "For the Lord, himself, shall descend from heaven with a shout, with the voice of the archangel, and with the trump of God: and the dead in Christ shall rise first: Then we which are alive and remain shall be caught up together with them in the clouds, to meet the Lord in the air: and so shall we ever be with the Lord."]*

This event, described here, refers to the catching up of the church from the earth to meet the Lord in the air. It involves only the faithful of Christ's churches.

> *[Watch therefore: for ye know not what hour your Lord doth come. But know this, that if the good man of the house had known in what watch the thief would come, he would have watched, and would not have suffered his house to be broken up. Therefore, be ye also ready: for in such an hour as ye think not the Son of man cometh. Matt. 24:42-44.]*

Watch there: for ye know not what hour your Lord doth come. Christ's warns in these verses that His disciples must always be ready for His coming must be understood as referring to His return from heaven to take church saints out of the world.

Jesus explicitly states that His coming for the saints living before the tribulation will be at an unexpected time and without warning. He declares that they not only "know not" the time, but that He will return at a time when they "think not the Son of Man cometh." This clearly points to an element of surprise, amazement, and unexpectedness for the faithful at this particular return of Christ.

Christ's coming at an unknown time is to be as unexpected as that of a thief who breaks into a house. Thus, the devoted disciple must be ready at any time for the appearance of the Lord.

> *[Then shall the kingdom of heaven be likened unto ten virgins, which took their lamps, and went forth to meet the bridegroom. And five of them were wise, and five were foolish. They that were foolish took their lamps, and took no oil with them: but the wise took oil in their vessels with their lamps. Matt. 25:1-4].*

Jesus gave the following parables to clarify further what it means to be ready for His return and how to live until He comes. In the story of the bridesmaids, we are taught that every person is responsible for his or her own spiritual condition. The story of the talents shows the necessity of using well what God has entrusted to us. The parable of the sheep and goats stresses the importance of serving others in need.

This parable is about a wedding. On the wedding day, the bridegroom went to the bride's house for the ceremony. Then, the bride and groom, along with a great parade, returned to the groom's house where a feast took place, lasting a full week.

These virgins (bridesmaids) were waiting for the parade, and they hoped to take part in the wedding banquet. But when the groom did not come at the expected time, five of them were out of lamp oil. By the time they had purchased extra oil, it was too late to join the feast.

When Jesus returned to take his people to heaven, we must be ready. Spiritual preparation cannot be bought or borrowed at the last minute. Our relationship with God must be our own.

I dreamed three months later the same angel came back to me in a dream, lifted my spirit from my body, and took me to Heaven's doors. I could feel my spirit going through the clouds. We got to this big door, pretty door as white as snow; it looked like a big pearl. He opens it for me, I was going to walk in, but the angel would not let me. He told me to look in the door. This dream was so anointed, so awesome! I saw the people that were in heaven, not their faces, only their backs. They all were dressed in white robes. I looked at the floor and the walls. They looked like pure gold, clear like glass. It hurt my eyes to look around; everything was so bright! I asked the angel where was God. He told me that God was on the throne and I could see Him when I came back. This place was so awesome! Would I want to spend eternity there? YES!

Someone ask the question what is heaven? Heaven is where God is. "All spiritual blessings in heavenly places" means all the good things God gives us-salvation, the gifts of the Spirit. Power to do God's will, the hope of living forever with Christ. Because we have an intimate relationship with Christ, we can enjoy these blessings now.

God's purpose is to offer salvation to the world, just as he planned to do long ago. God is sovereign; he is in charge. When your life seems chaotic, rest in this truth: Jesus is Lord, and God is in control. His purpose to save you cannot be thwarted, no matter what evil Satan may bring.

When we left heaven that night in my dream, he took me to a well in the ground, put me in that well which was HELL, I went down, down, I began to scream, it was offer I was crying please take me out of this dark place but he didn't. I went so far down I began to see a little dim light. It smelled so bad, it made me sick, I saw fire burning, people was crying and screaming out so sad asking God to please have mercy on them. I screamed at this angel please take him out of this Hell. There were so much screaming and it smelled so bad. I saw someone covered with big worms while engulfed with fire. Every where I looked fire was burning people up. This place was awful I do not want anyone to go there. In my dream I did not see it all, I just saw enough to tell people that HELL is bad.

I was screaming to this angle telling him to please take me out of this place, I remember saying Lord please have mercy on me, I went back up to the earth when I asked the Lord to have mercy on me. That was awful. The smell was so bad. Would I want to go back? NO!

The wicked shall be turned into Hell and all the nations that forget God and in hell he lifts up his eyes, being in torments, and seeth Abraham afar off and Lazarus in his bosom. And he cried and said, Father Abraham, have mercy on me, and send Lazarus, that he may dip the tip of his finger in water, and cool my tongue; for I am tormented in this flame (St. Luke 16:23-24).

Someone may ask, what is heaven? Heaven is where God is. "All spiritual blessings in heavenly places" means all the good things God givens us- salvation, the gifts of the Spirit, power to do God's will, the hope of living forever with Christ. Because we have an intimate relationship with Christ, we can enjoy these blessings now.

As believers, we are "strangers and pilgrims" in this world because our real home is with God. Heaven is not the pink-cloud-and-harp existence popular in cartoons. Heaven is where God dwells. It operates according to God's principles and values, and it is eternal and unshakable. It came in a fuller way in the person of Jesus Christ, "God with us." It permeated the entire world as the Holy Spirit came to dwell in the heart of every believer. Someday, after God judges and destroys all sin, the Kingdom of heaven will rule every corner of this earth. John saw this day in a vision, and he cried out, "Behold, the tabernacle of God is with men, and he will dwell with them, and they shall be his people, and God himself shall be with them, and be their God." Our real home, our true loyalty, should not be to this earth because it will be destroyed. Our loyalty should be to God's truth, his way of life, and his dedicated people. Because of this, we often feel like strangers in a world that would prefer to ignore God.

After this I looked, and, behold, a door was opened in heaven: and the first voice which I *heard was as it were of a trumpet talking with me; which said, Come up hither, and I will shew thee things which must be hereafter [Rev. 4:1].*

Here we get a glimpse of Christ's glory. We see into the throne room of heaven. God is on the throne and orchestrating all the events that John will record. The world is not spinning out of control; the God of creation will carry out his plans as Christ initiates the final battle with the forces of evil. John shows us heaven before showing us earth so we will not be frightened by future events.

"Hell," the place of unquenchable fire, is so terrible that every influence of sin must be opposed and rejected, whatever the cost. Sin must be put to death; we must never stop waging war against it through the Spirit. Everyone will be salted with fire in one of two ways: (1) either by fiery tribulation in this life that comes to those who genuinely follow Jesus Christ; or (2) by the fire of hell in the next life that comes to those who reject Jesus in this life.

The rich man's life is consumed in self-centered living. He made the wrong choice and suffered eternally. Lazarus lived all his life in poverty, but his heart was right with God. His name means "God is my help," and he never gave up his faith in God. He died and was immediately taken to Paradise with Abraham. The destinies of both men were irreversible at death.

And death and hell were cast into the lake of fire. This is the second death (Rev. 20:14). The Bible portrays a terrible picture of the destiny of the lost. It speaks of "tribulation and anguish" (Rom. 2:9), "weeping and gnashing of teeth" (Matt. 22:13; 25:30), "everlasting destruction" (2 Thes. 1:9), and a "furnace of fire" (Matt. 13:42, 50). It speaks of "chains of darkness" (2 Pet. 2:4), "everlasting punishment" (Matt. 25:46), a "hell" and a "fire that never shall be quenched" (Mark 9:43), a "lake of fire burning with brimstone," and "the smoke of their torment ascendeth up for ever and ever: and they have no rest day nor night"

It has been a long and up hill journey, but God has been right by my side. When I didn't think that I would make it God was right there. I have been preaching and teaching for three years.

> *Whither shall I go from thy spirit? or whither shall I flee from thy presence? If I ascend up into heaven, thou are there: If I make my bed in hell, behold, thou art there. If I take the wings of the morning, and dwell in the uttermost parts of the sea; Even there shall Thy hand lead me, and thy right hand shall hold me (Psalm 139:7-10).*

The Bible teaches that one's existence does not end at death but continues on forever, either in the presence of God or in a place of punishment. Jesus teaches that there is a place of eternal punishment for those condemned before God. It is the terrifying reality of continuous punishment, the place of a "fire that never shall be quenched, of everlasting fire, prepared for the devil and his angels" of "wailing and gnashing of teeth," of binding and outer darkness, and of torment and anguish and separation from heaven. The Bible teaches that judgment on evildoers is certain. The main idea is condemnation, suffering, and separation from God with no time limit. Christians may find this doctrine unpleasant or hard to understand. Yet we must submit to the authority of God's Word and trust God's decision and justice.

We must keep foremost in our thinking that God sent His Son to die in order that no one will perish. It is not God's intention or desire to send anyone to hell. Those who enter hell do so by resisting the salvation provided by God. The face and reality of hell should cause all of God's people to hate sin fervently, to seek continually the salvation of the lost, and to warn everyone of the future righteous judgment of God.

The child of God can never move beyond God's care, guidance, and supporting strength. He is with us in all situations, in whatever the present and the future brings.

Jesus said, "The Spirit of the Lord is upon Me, because He hath anointed Me to preach the gospel to the poor; He hath sent Me to heal the brokenhearted, to preach deliverance to the captives, and recovering of sight to the blind, to set at liberty them that are bruised" (Luke 4:18).

Jesus identifies with my pain and suffering. When I reached out to Him He allow the Holy Spirit to have His way, His anointing is always present to deliver. He knows what it is like to suffer at the hands of others. Once you have called out to Him, you can lift up your hands in praise. No matter what I had suffered, I can hold up my head. Regardless of who has hurt me?

When you have suffered, it makes you able to relate to other people's pain. The Lord settled me in a ministry that just tends to cater to hurting people. Sometimes when I minister, I find myself fighting back tears. Some times, I can hear the cries of anguished people in the crowd.

Satan's power is not eternal-he will meet his doom. He began his evil work in mankind at the beginning and continues it today, but he will be destroyed when he is thrown into the lake of fire. Satan will be released from the bottomless pit ["his prison,"], but he will never be released from the lake of fire. He will never be a threat to anyone again.

At the judgment, the books will be opened. The book of life contains the names of those who have put their trust in Christ to save them. And the dead were judged out of those things which were written in the books, according to their works.

The effects of sin, such as sorrow, pain, unhappiness, and death are gone forever, for the evil things of the first heaven and earth have completely passed away. Believers, although remembering all things worth remembering, will evidently not remember that which would cause them sorrow.

God Himself declares who shall inherit the blessings of the new heaven and the new earth—those who faithfully persevere as Christ's over comers. Those who do not overcome sin and ungodliness will be cast into the fire.

> *AND HE showed me a pure river of water of life, clear as crystal proceeding out of the throne of God and of the Lamb. In the midst of the street of it, and on either side of the river, was there the tree of life, which bare twelve manners of fruits, and yielded her fruit every month:* and the leaves of the tree were for the healing of the nations [Rev. 22:1-2].

The tree refers to the eternal life given to all who populate the new city. The healing leaves indicate the absence of anything that brings physical or spiritual harm, our new bodies we will be dependent on the Lord for life, strength, and health. The water of life is a symbol of eternal life. Jesus used this same image with the Samaritan woman. It pictures the fullness of life with God and the eternal blessings that come when we believe in him and satisfy our spiritual thirst.

This tree of life is like the tree of life in the Garden of Eden. After Adam and Eve sinned, they were forbidden to eat from the tree of life because they could not have eternal life as long as they were under sin's control. But because of the forgiveness of sin through the blood of Jesus, there will be no evil or sin in this city. We will be able to eat freely from the tree of life when sin's control over us is destroyed and our eternity with God is secure.

Someone may think why the nations need to be healed if all evil is gone. Where is the water flowing from the Temple that produces trees with healing leaves? I am not implying that there will be illness in the new earth; I am emphasizing that the water of life produces health and strength wherever it goes.

> *And by the river upon the bank thereof, on this side and on that side, shall grow all trees for meat, whose leaf shall not fade, neither shall the fruit thereof be consumed: it shall* bring *forth new fruit according to his months, because their waters they issued out of the sanctuary: and the fruit thereof shall be for meat, and the leaf thereof for medicine [Ezekiel 47:12].*

The river symbolizes life from God and the blessings that follow from his throne *And they shall see his face; and his name shall be in their foreheads [Rev. 22:4].*

May I tell you this is the final goal of redemptive history; God is dwelling in the midst of His faithful people on a new earth purged from all evil. On this new earth the saints will see and dwell with Jesus, the Lamb of God, who through love redeemed them by His death on the cross. Their greatest happiness will be: "Blessed are the pure in heart; for they shall see God"

> *He which testifieth these things saith, Surely I come quickly. Amen. Even so, come, Lord Jesus. The grace of our Lord Jesus Christ be with you all. Amen [Rev. 22:20-21].*

The Bible ends with Jesus' promise that He is coming quickly, to which John responds.

"Come, Lord Jesus." This longing is shared by all true Christians. (1) This prayer is a confession that until He comes, our redemption remains incomplete, evil and sin are not yet overthrown, and this world is not yet renewed. (2) We have every reason to believe that the day is fast approaching when He who is called "The Word of God" and "the bright and morning star" will become LORD OF LORDS." This is our unfailing hope and joyful expectation. Down from heaven to take His faithful away from the earth to His Father's house, after which He will return in glory and triumph to reign forever as "KING OF KINGS, AND LORD

Many people don't want to believe that God sentences people to hell ("eternal fire") for rejecting Him, but this is clearly taught in Scripture. Sinners who don't seek forgiveness from God will face eternal separation from him.

Don't Waste The Grace

God gives a gift to each member of the body of Christ there ought not to be the distinction between the pulpit and the pew that we make. We are all workers together, and as workers of God, we should not receive God's grace in vain.

God gives us grace sufficient for our needs each day and He gives us that grace everyday that love and favor. Paul says do not waste the grace God has given us; do not receive God's grace in vain. Do not reject his grace in order to nurture frustrations and your disappointment. Every child of God is responsible to get out the Word of God as the preachers are.

I received the gift of preaching, you may be a schoolteacher, doctor or truck driver, a homemaker, but you are responsible today to get out the Word of God. We put too much on the preacher, everybody have a job. The shepherds do not produce sheep. Sheep produce sheep. God has given teachers, preachers, and evangelists and missionaries to fill out and prepare the body of believers so that those who are sitting in the pews might be equipped for their ministry of going out to witness for Christ.

The shepherd does not produce the sheep, they feed the sheep and he or she watches over the sheep. The pastor shepherds the sheep.

Paul unquestionably believed that a believer could receive the grace of God and experience salvation, and afterwards through spiritual carelessness or deliberate sin, abandon the faith and life of the gospel and again be lost. All people must be exhorted to be reconciled to God and to receive His grace. Those who receive God's grace must be exhorted not to receive it in vain.

Grace is God's presence, favor, and power. It is a force, a heavenly strength bestowed on those who call upon God. This grace will descend upon the faithful believer who accepts his weaknesses and difficulties for the gospel's sake. The greater our weakness and trials for Christ, the more grace God will give us to accomplish His will. What he bestows on us is always sufficient for us to live our daily lives, to work for Him, and to endure our suffering and "thorns in the flesh." As long as we draw near to Christ, Christ will bestow His heavenly strength and comfort on us. We should glorify and see eternal value in our weaknesses, for they cause the power of Christ to descend on us and dwell within us as we walk through life toward our heavenly home.

In my Christian journal I have learned to walk it as humble as I know how, my daddy always told me that God did not like proud, if you are proud then God can not use you. He taught me to have a humble spirit. It should be impressed upon our hearts and minds how much God hates pride. Pride in our lives will cause God to turn from our prayers and withhold His presence and grace from us. To be exalted in our own minds and to seek honor and the esteem of others in order to satisfy our pride is to shut out the help of God. But for those who humbly submit themselves to God and draw near to Him there is abundant grace, mercy, and help in every situation of life.

The whole movement of the Christian life from beginning to end is dependent on this grace. God gives a measure of grace as a gift to unbelievers in order that they may be able to believe on the Lord Jesus. God's grace must be diligently desired and sought after. Some of the ways by which God's grace is received are: studying and obeying the Holy Scriptures; hearing the proclamation of the gospel; praying; fasting; worshiping Christ; being continually filled with the Holy Spirit; and participating in the Lord's Supper.

God could have left us spiritually dead, in rebellion against him an in bondage to our sins. But he didn't save us because of, but rather in spite of, what he saw in us. In addition to thanking him for what he has done for us, we should also show humble patience and tolerance for others who seem unworthy or undeserving of our love and compassion. They may be spiritually dull, rebellious, and even antagonistic toward God. So were we; *but God loved us anyway.* Can we do less for fellow sinners?

"The Word was made flesh" means becoming human. By doing so, Christ became the perfect teacher-in Jesus' life, we see how God thinks and therefore how we should think. The perfect example-as a model of what we are to become, he shows us how to live and gives us the power to live that way; the perfect sacrifice-Jesus came as a sacrifice for all sins, and his death satisfied God's requirement for the removal of sin.

"The only begotten of the Father" means Jesus is God's only and unique Son. The emphasis is on unique. Jesus is one of a kind and enjoys a relationship with God unlike all believers who are called "sons and daughters" and said to be "born of God." When Christ was conceived, God became a man. He was not part man and part God; he was completely human and completely divine. Before Christ came, people could know God partially. After Christ came, people could know God fully because he became visible and tangible in Christ. Christ is the perfect expression of God in human form. The two most common errors people make about Jesus are to minimize his humanity or to minimize his divinity. Jesus is both God and man.

Now to him that worketh is the reward not reckoned of grace, but of debt? But to him that worketh not, but believeth on him that justifieth the ungodly, his faith is counted for righteousness (Romans 4:4-5).

This verse means that if a person could earn right standing with God by being good, the granting of that gift wouldn't be a free act; it would be an obligation. Our self-reliance is futile; all we can do is cast ourselves on God's mercy and grace. Some people, when they learn that we are saved by God through faith, start to worry. "Do I have enough faith?" they wonder. "Is my faith strong enough to save me?" These people miss the point. It is Jesus Christ who saves us, not our feelings or actions, and he is strong enough to save us no matter how weak our faith is. Jesus offers us salvation as a gift, because he loves us, not because we have earned it through our powerful faith.

What then, is the role of faith? Faith is belief and trusting in Jesus Christ, reaching out to accept his wonderful gift of salvation.

I wish that I could perform a miraculous act that would convince everyone once and for all that Jesus is the Lord. If I could perform a miracle, it wouldn't convince everyone. God gave Paul and Barnabas power to do great miracles as proof, but people were still divided. Don't spend your time and energy wishing for miracles. Sow your seeds of Good News on the best ground you can find in the best way you can, and leave the convincing to the Holy Spirit.

Being justified freely by his grace through the redemption that is in Christ Jesus: (Romans 3:24). "Justified freely" means to be declared not guilty. When a judge in a court of law declares the defendant not guilty, all the charges are removed from his record. Legally, it is as if the person had never been accused. When God forgives our sins, our record is wiped clean. It is as though we had never sinned.

As a sinner, separated from God, you see his Law from below, as a ladder to be climbed to get to God. Perhaps you have repeatedly tried to climb it, only to fall to the ground every time you have advanced one or two runs. Or perhaps the sheer height of the ladder seems so overwhelming that you have never even started up. In either case, what relief you should feel to see Jesus offering with open arms to lift you above the ladder of the Law, to take you directly to God! Once Jesus lifts you into God's presence, you are free to obey—out of love, not necessity, and through God's power, not your own. You know that if you stumble, you will not fall back to the ground. Instead, you will be caught and held in Jesus' loving arms.

But by the grace of God I am what I am: and his grace which was bestowed upon me was not in vain; but I laboured more abundantly than they all; yet not I, but the grace of God which was with me (1 Cor. 25:10).

As a zealous Pharisee, Paul had been an enemy of the Christian church-even to the point of capturing and persecuting believers. Thus, he felt unworthy to be called an apostle of Christ. Though undoubtedly, the most influential of the apostles, Paul was deeply humble. He knew he had worked hard and accomplished much but only because God had poured kindness and grace upon him. True humility is not convincing yourself that you are worthless but recognizing God's work in you. It is having God's perspective on who you are and acknowledging his grace in developing your abilities.

God could have left us spiritually dead, in rebellion against him and in bondage to our sins. But he didn't. He did not save us because of, but rather in spite of, what he saw in us. In addition to thanking him for what he has done for us, we should also show humble patience and tolerance for others who seem unworthy or undeserving of our love and compassion. They may be spiritually dull, rebellious, and even antagonistic toward God. So were we; but God loved us anyway. Can we do less for fellow sinners?

When we tell others about Christ, it is important always to be gracious in what we say. No matter how much sense the message makes, we lose our effectiveness if we are not courteous. Just as we like to be respected, we must respect others if we want them to listen to what we have to say.

Not only is the believer said to be saved by grace, but he is said to "stand" in grace. The word stand, as used in the New Testament, gives expression to the thought of continuing and enduring, and to "stand" in grace is to abide unchanged, to endure, and to continue in grace. We read: "We have access by faith into this grace wherein we stand" (Rom. 5:2), and, "This is the true grace of God wherein ye stand" (1 Pet. 5:12).

The continued exercise of divine grace toward the Christian is the one and only basis upon which one may hope to endure, for, as certainly as grace is the one and only basis upon which God can save a meritless sinner, so certainly grace alone is the basis upon which God can righteously keep one saved. Having begun in the Spirit, or wholly in the power and grace of God, there is no hope for continuance to be found in the flesh, or in the resources of human strength. Human ability can no more maintain a right standing before God than it can attain such a standing.

Since the application of divine grace for the salvation of the sinner precedes, in point of time, the application of that grace for the keeping of the one who is saved, it is perhaps permissible to contemplate the operation of divine grace in a twofold classification-the grace which saves, and the grace which keeps. But, on the other hand, an overemphasis of this twofold classification is misleading in the extreme, for in no sense are there two efforts, or operations, of divine grace. The keeping ministry of God in grace is but the realization of that which is purposed, programmed, and wholly provided for in His saving ministry in grace. In reality, God offers no saving ministry of grace which does not include and guarantee His keeping ministry of grace. The varied operations of divine grace in behalf of the sinner, which contemplate his every need to the end of eternity, are one indivisible purpose of God.

Grace may be extended to the unsaved on the basis of the fact that Christ has already borne the condemnation of his sin, so certainly grace may be extended and continued to the saved on the basis of the fact that Christ has already borne the condemnation of the Christian's sin. In this dispensation, the unsaved are not said to be condemned primarily because of their sins which Christ has borne; they are condemned because they do not believe on Christ who bore their sins. "He that believeth not is condemned already, because he hath not believed in the name of the only begotten Son of God" (John 3:18). In like manner, the Christian will never be condemned because of the sin which Christ has borne. So, also, the Christian, having accepted Christ, can never be condemned for lack of saving faith. It is therefore said: "Verily, verily, I say unto you, He that heareth my word, and believeth on him that hath sent me, hath everlasting life, and shall not come into condemnation; but is passed from death unto life"(John 5:24). "There is therefore now no condemnation to them that are in Christ Jesus" (Rom. 8:1, R.V.). "He that believeth on him is not condemned" (John 3:18).

But grow in the grace and knowledge of our Lord and Savior Jesus Christ [2 Peter 3:18].

The Scriptures reveal four stages of spiritual growth in the Christian life: (1) The baby stage. A baby thinks only of self; and, if denied the things desired, it will raise a rumpus. It seeks its own; its feelings are easily hurt and it is often jealous. A baby lives to be served-it never serves. It drinks milk, and cannot eat strong meat. It cries, but never sings. It tries to talk, but never makes sense. These infant characteristics are so prominent in the lives of many church members. They have been born into the family of God, but have failed to develop spiritually. They are spiritual babies-carnal Christians. (2) The little child. Some Christians grow to be little children spiritually, but stop there. Here are some of the characteristics of children: they are often untruthful, envious, and cruel. Is rebuked, they become martyrs; if crossed, they are resentful and often make a scene. They are talebearers, repeating everything they hear (in adults it is called gossip). They are given to emotional outbursts, and are easily puffed up. They love praise, and will accept it from any source. They seek only the things that appeal to self. Are you a spiritual child? (3) The young man. Spiritual growth to that of a young man is not reached by many. He is strong and virile and is well able to overcome his enemy. He has a vision for the future and the faith and courage to tackle it. He is preparing for his productive years. You, too, can become a young man or woman spiritually by "[putting] away childish things" and grow. (4) The father stage. This stage of spiritual development can be reach by all, but so few ever attain it. The spiritual father has peace with God. He knows the peace of God. He rejoices in his spiritual children. He has learned contentment under all circumstances. He knows the only source of true strength. He does not brood over the past, but looks to the future. He knows that all things work together in his of her eternal good. He enjoys abundant life now and will enjoy it in the life to come.

Grace is the love and mercy of God in action. Mercy is negative, and love is positive; both together mean grace. To show mercy in love is grace. God showed mercy in love when He sent His Son to bear our sins in His own body on the cross.

(1) The grace of God saves forever.
(2) The grace of God is unconditional; that is, we are not saved on the condition that we "hold out until the end" or that we "fail not" or that we "do our best." We are saved by the grace of God, apart from works.
(3) The grace of God is sufficient.

(4) The grace of God makes no discrimination.
(5) The grace of God justifies.
(6) The grace of God makes every believer an heir.
(7) The grace of God teaches the believer how to live.

The grace of God is nothing less than the unlimited love of God expressed in the gift of His Son, our Savior. It is the undeserved love of God toward sinners.

For by grace you have been saved through faith, and that not of yourselves; it is the gift of God. Not of works, lest anyone should boast (Ephesians 2:8-9). Just remember that grace is God's voluntary and loving favor given to those he saves. We can't earn it, nor do we deserve it. No religious or moral effort can gain it, for it comes only from God's mercy and love. Without God's grace, no person can be saved.

Grace is God's free gift of salvation given to us in Christ. Receiving it bring us peace. In a world of noise, confusion, and relentless pressures, people long for peace. Many give up the search, thinking it impossible to find, but true peace of heart and mind is available to us through faith in Jesus Christ.

When our will is weak, when our reason is confused, when our conscience is burdened with a load of guilt, we must remember that God cares for us continually, and his mercies never fail. When friends and family desert us, when coworkers don't understand us, when we are tired of being good, God's mercies never fail. When we can't see the way or seem to hear God's voice, when we lack courage to go on, God's mercies never fail. When our shortcomings beset us and awareness of our sins overcomes us, God's mercies never fail.

Jesus was touched with compassion and pity for the needs and suffering of humanity. Jesus is the same today. He is moved with a deep and earnest sympathy by the needs and hurts of each child of God. This assures us that in our troubles we can draw near to Him in prayer in order to receive grace, mercy and help.

> *But grow in the grace and knowledge of our Lord and Savior Jesus Christ. To Him be the glory both now and forever. Amen [2 Peter 3:18].*

The Scriptures reveal four stages of spiritual growth in the Christian life.

(1) The baby stage. A baby thinks only of self; and, if denied the things desired, it will raise a rumpus. It seeks its own; its feelings are easily hurt and it is often jealous. A baby lives to be served-it never serves. It drinks milk, and cannot eat strong meat. It cries, but never sings. It tries to talk, but never makes sense. These infant characteristics are so prominent in the lives of many church members. They have been born into the family of God, but have failed to develop spiritually. They are spiritual babies-carnal Christians.

(2) The little child. Some Christians grow to be little children spiritually, but stop there. Here are some of the characteristics of children: they are often untruthful, envious, and cruel. If rebuked, they become martyrs; if crossed, they are resentful and often make a scene. They are talebearers, repeating everything they hear (in adults it is called gossip). They are given to emotional outbursts, and are easily puffed up. They love praise, and will accept it from any source. They seek only the things that appeal to self. Are you a spiritual child?

(3) The young man stage. Spiritual growth to that of a young man is not reached by many. He is strong and virile and is well able to overcome his enemy. He has a vision for the future and the faith and courage to tackle it. He is preparing for his productive years. You, too, can become a young man spiritually by "[putting] away childish things," and grow.

(4) The father stage. This stage of spiritual development can be reached by all, but so few ever Attain it. The spiritual father has peace with God. He knows the peace of God. He rejoices in his spiritual children. He has learned contentment under all circumstances. He knows the only source of true strength. He does not brood over the past, but looks to the future. He knows that all things work together in his life for his eternal good. He enjoys abundant life now and will enjoy it in the life to come.

BEING REJECTED IN YOUR COMMUNITY

It is sad to realize, but often people who knew you way back when, do not have the ability to know you now. Jesus did not do many miracles in his home town. He held back because of the limited vision of those who were more acquainted with his past than his present. They recognized his "wisdom" and observed his "miracles," but their opinion reverted to what they had known of him before. Jesus responded to that by leaving. He could have done more had they had faith.

Some of you are being held back by an "I-knew-you-when" people. They keep you stuck in a stage of your life that is past and gone. These people define you on the basis of who you were, not who you have become, and certainly not who you can someday be.

These I-knew-you-when people they do not permit you to embrace the future because they want to keep you in the past. God wants to do great things in you, but you need to move beyond the I-knew-you-when people.

We cannot overcome the Devil ourselves; we are no match for the Devil. We are not even told to fight the Devil; we are told that God will fight for us.

Let me call your attention to the fact that in Christ's day they never questioned whether or not He could perform miracles. They wanted to know where does He get His wisdom, and how can He do these mighty works? "Is not this the carpenter's son?" That was what confused them. They did not recognize who He really was. To them

He was just a carpenter's son. And that is all He is to some folk in our day. They think He was a great teacher, a great man, a wonderful person, but to them He was only a carpenter's son.

It is obvious that the Lord Jesus had brothers and sisters of course, they were half brothers and half sisters, younger than He was, and born of Mary and Joseph. They did not understand until after His resurrection that He was truly the Son of God.

And they were offended in him. But Jesus said unto them, A prophet is not without honour, save in his own country, and in his own house (Matt. 13:57). You see, His home town folk were so familiar with Him and with His family that they were "offended in him." That is, they took offense at Him. I suppose they said. "We know His family. He grew up among us. Where does He get the things He teaches?"

This is a tremendous revelation. Note what it was that limited the power of God when He was here. It was unbelief! "He did not do many mighty works there because of their unbelief." It was not that He was unable to do them; but because of their unbelief, He did very few miracles there. The great problem with you and I is that we do not have faith for the salvation of men and women. We need the kind of faith that believes Christ can save the lost.

He is limited today in your own community, in your church, in your family, and in your own life by **unbelief.** And this is certainly true of me also. Our Lord states a great truth here.

My people are destroyed for lack of knowledge: because thou hast rejected knowledge, I will also reject thee, that thou shalt be no priest to me: seeing thou hast forgotten the law of thy God, I will also forget thy children (Hosea 4:6).

The lack of personal knowledge of God was destroying the people, but not because knowledge was not available. The people were willfully rejecting the truth God had given them through the prophets and His written Word. Even today within the church, some are being destroyed by the sinful ways of the world because they do not know God and His inspired Word.

He is despised and rejected of men; a man of sorrows, and acquainted with grief: and we hide as it were our faces from him; he was despised, and we esteemed him not (Isaiah 53:5).

Instead of being accepted by Israel, Jesus Christ would be hated and rejected by its rulers. These are words being comfort to believers who are experiencing great affliction or adversity. When we are weighed down by trials and shaken by the tempests of life's circumstances, we must remember that these are the very conditions that cause our Lord to have compassion upon us and to draw near to us so that we may be spiritually strengthened.

Jesus' brothers had a difficult time believing in him. Some of these brothers would eventually become leaders in the church, but for several years they were embarrassed by him. After Jesus died and rose again, they finally believed. We today have every reason to believe because we have the full record of Jesus' miracles, death, and resurrection. We also have the evidence of what the Gospel has done in people's lives through the centuries. Do not miss this opportunity to believe in God's Son.

The world hated Jesus. We who follow him can expect that many people will hate us as well. If circumstances are going to well, ask if you are following him as you should. We can be grateful if life goes well, but not at the cost of following Jesus halfheartedly or not at all.

Jesus came with the greatest gift ever offered, so why did he often act secretly? I believe religious leaders hated him, they refused his gifts of salvation no matter what he said or did. The more he taught and worked publicly, the more these leaders would cause trouble for Jesus and his followers. So it was necessary for Jesus to teach and work as quietly as possible. Many people today have the privilege of teaching, preaching, and worshiping publicly with little persecution. These believers should thankfully take advantage of their freedom.

Many church people talk about Jesus! But when it came time to speak up for him in public, no one said a word. All are afraid. Fear can stifle our witness. Although many people talk about Christ in church, when it comes to making a public statement about their faith, they are often embarrassed. Jesus says that he will acknowledge us before God if we acknowledge him before others.

Some of the people grumbled in disagreement because they could not accept Jesus' claim of divinity. They saw him only as a carpenter from Nazareth. They refused to believe he was God's divine Son, and they could not tolerate his message. Many people reject Christ because they say they could not believe he is the Son of God. In reality, the claims he makes for their loyalty and obedience are what they can't accept. So to protect themselves from the message, they deny the messenger.

I have learned that God plays the most active role in our salvation not man. When someone chooses to believe in Jesus Christ as Savior, he does so only in response to the urging of God's Holy Spirit. God does the urging; then we decide whether or not to believe. No one can believe in Jesus without God's help.

As a youngster, Joseph was overconfident. His natural self-assurance, increased by being Jacob's favorite son and by knowing of God's designs on his life, was unbearable to his ten older brothers, who eventually conspired against him. But this self-assurance, molded by pain and combined with a personal knowledge of God, allowed him to survive and prosper where most would have failed. He added quiet wisdom to his confidence and won the hearts of everyone he met—Potiphar, the jailer, other prisoners, the pharaoh, and after many years, even those ten brothers.

I can identify with one or more of these hardships Joseph experienced: I was betrayed and deserted by some of my family and many of my friends. Joseph was exposed to sexual temptation, and punished for doing the right thing; he endured a long imprisonment and was forgotten by those he helped. As you read his story, note what Joseph did in each case. His positive response transformed the setback into a step forward. He didn't spend much time asking "Why?" His approach was "What shall I do now?" Those who met Joseph were aware that wherever he went and whatever he did, God was with him. When you're facing a setback, the beginning of a Joseph-like attitude is to acknowledge that God is with you. There is nothing like his presence to shed new light on a dark situation.

Joseph's brothers were already angry over the possibility of being ruled by their brother. Joseph then fueled the fire with his immature and boastful manner. No one enjoys a braggart. Joseph learned this the hard way. His angry brothers sold him into slavery to get rid of him. After several years of hardship, Joseph learned an important lesson: Because our talents and knowledge come from God, it is more appropriate to thank him for them than to brag about them. Later Joseph gave God the credit.

Could jealousy ever make you feel like killing someone? Before saying, "Of course not," look at what happened in this story. Ten men were willing to kill their brother over a coat and because of his dreams. Their deep jealousy had grown into ugly rage, blinding them completely to what was right. Jealousy can be hard to recognize, because our reasons for it seem to make sense. But left unchecked, jealousy grows quickly and leads to serious sins. The longer you cultivate jealous feelings, the harder it is to uproot them. The time to deal with jealousy is when you notice yourself keeping score of others' recognition, awards, and achievements.

God alone has the right to be jealous and to carry out vengeance. Jealousy and vengeance may be surprising terms to associate with God. When humans are jealous and take vengeance, they are usually acting in a spirit of selfishness. But it is appropriate for God to insist on our complete allegiance, and it is just for him to punish unrepentant evildoers. His jealousy and vengeance are unmixed with selfishness. Their purpose is to remove sin and restore peace to the world.

God is slow to angry, but when he is ready to punish, even the earth trembles. Often people avoid God because they see evildoers in the world and hypocrites in the church. They don't realize that because God is slow to anger, he gives his true followers time to share his love and truth with evildoers. But judgment will come; God will not allow sin to go unchecked forever. When people wonder why God doesn't punish evil immediately, help them remember that if he did, none of us would be here. We can all be thankful that God gives people time to turn to him. To those who refuse to believe, God's punishment is like an angry fire. To those who love him, his mercy is security and peace, supplying all our needs without diminishing his supply. But to his enemies he is a flood that will sweep them away. The relationship we have is up to us.

> *I said, surely thou wilt fear me, thou wilt receive instruction; so their dwelling should not be cut off, howsoever I punished them: but they rose early, and corrupted all their doings [Zephaniah 3:7]*

When God teaches, he expects us to listen and learn. If we do not learn, he must punish us in order to teach us. God doesn't want us to suffer, but he will continue to chasten us until we learn the lesson he has for us. Be teachable, not unreachable.

Many people believe that to survive in this world a person must be tough, strong, unbending, and harsh. But God says, "Not by might, nor by power, but by my spirit." The key words are, "by my spirit." It is only through God's Spirit that anything of lasting value is accomplished. The returned exiles were indeed weak-harassed by their enemies, tired, discouraged, and poor. But actually they had God on their side! As you live for God, determine not to trust in your own strength or abilities. Instead, depend on God and work in the power of his Spirit. God promises to strengthen his people. When we stay closely connected to him, his Spirit enables us to do his will, despite the obstacles. When we stray away from him, we are cut off from our power source.

The brothers were worried about bearing the guilt or Joseph's death. Judah suggested an option that was not right, but would leave them innocent of murder. Sometimes we jump at a solution because it is the lesser of two evils but still is not the right action to take. When someone proposes a seemingly workable solution, first ask, "Is it right?"

Although Joseph's brothers didn't kill him outright, they probably didn't expect him to survive for long as a slave. My friends were not for me I thought that I would not survive, but when God is on your side He will bring you through. Joseph's brothers thought they would never see him again. But God was in control of Joseph's life and had other plans.

> *I was a reproach among all mine enemies, but especially among my neighbours, and a fear to mine acquaintance: they that did see me without fled from me (Psalm 31-13).*

David describes the helplessness and hopelessness we feel when we are hated or rejected. But adversity is easier to accept when we recognize our true relationship with the sovereign God. Although our enemies may seem to have the upper hand, they are ultimately the helpless and hopeless ones. Those who know God will be victorious in the end. We can have courage today because God will preserve us.

> *And, behold, the whole city came out to meet Jesus: and when they saw him, they besought him that he would depart out of their coasts (Matt. 8:34).*

Why did the people ask Jesus to leave? Unlike their pagan gods, Jesus could not be contained, controlled, or appeased. They feared Jesus' supernatural power, a power they had never before witnessed. And they were upset about losing a herd of pigs more than they were glad about the deliverance of the devil possessed men. Are you more concerned about property and programs than people? Human beings are created in God's image and have eternal value. How foolish and yet how easy it is to value possessions, investments, and even animals above human life. Would you rather have Jesus leave you than finish his work in you?

Jesus' first words to Simon Peter were "Come ye after me." His last words to him were "Follow thou me". Every step of the way between those two challenges, Peter never failed to follow—even though he often stumbled.

When Jesus entered Peter's life, this plain fisherman became a new person with new goals and new priorities. He did not become a perfect person, however, and he never stopped being Simon Peter. We may wonder what Jesus saw in Simon that made him greet this potential disciple with a new name, Peter—"the Rock." Impulsive Peter certainly didn't act like a rock much of the time. But when Jesus chose his followers, he wasn't looking for models, he was looking for men, he chose people who could be changed by his love, and then he sent them out to communicate that his acceptance was available to anyone-even to those who often fail.

We may wonder what Jesus sees in us when he calls us to follow him. But we know Jesus accepted Peter, and, in spite of his failures, Peter went on to do great things for God. Are you willing to keep following Jesus, even when you fail?

There were three stages to Peter's denial. First he acted confused and tried to divert attention from himself by changing the subject. Second, he denied Jesus with an oath. Third, he began to curse and swear. Believers who deny Christ often begin doing so subtly by pretending not to know him. When opportunities to discuss religious issues come up, they walk away or pretend they don't know the answers. With only a little more pressure, they can be induced to deny flatly their relationship with Christ. If you find yourself subtly avoiding occasions to talk about Christ, watch out. You may be on the road to denying him.

It is easy to get angry at the Jewish Council and the Roman governor for their injustice in condemning Jesus, but Peter and the rest of the disciples also contributed to Jesus' pain by deserting him. While most of us are not like the Jewish and Roman leaders, we are all like the disciples, for all of us have been guilty of denying Christ as Lord in vital areas of our lives. We may pride ourselves that we have not committed certain sins, but we are all guilty of sin. Don't try to excuse yourself by pointing at others whose sins seem worse than yours. All ways look at the man or woman in the mirror.

All the disciples declared that they would die rather than desert Jesus. A few hours later, however, they all scattered. Talk is cheap. It is easy to say we are devoted to Christ, but our claims are meaningful only when they are tested in the crucible of persecution. How strong is your faith? Is it strong enough to stand under intense trials? This was the second time that evening that Jesus predicted that his disciples would desert him.

In times of suffering people sometimes wish they knew the future, or they wish they could understand the reason for their anguish. Jesus knew what lay ahead of him, and he knew the reason.

Even so, his struggle was intense-more wrenching than any struggle we will ever have to face. What does it take to be able to say "Thy will be done"? It takes trust in God's plans, prayer, and obedience each step of the way.

Around the world, the Gospel has most often taken root in places prepared by the blood of martyrs. Before a person can give his life for the Gospel, however, he must first live his life for the Gospel. One way God trains his servants is to place them in insignificant positions. Their desire to serve Christ is translated into the reality of serving others. Stephen was an effective administrator and messenger before a martyr.

Stephen was named one of the managers of food distribution in the early church. Long before violent persecution broke out against Christians, there was already social ostracism. Jews who accepted Jesus as Messiah were usually cut off from their families. As a result, the believers depended on each other for support. The sharing of homes, food, and resources was both a practical and necessary mark of the early church. Eventually, the number of believers made it necessary to organize the sharing. People were being overlooked. There were complaints. Those chosen to help manage were chosen for their integrity, wisdom, and sensitivity to God.

Besides being a good administrator, Stephen was also a powerful speaker. When confronted in the Temple by various antagonistic groups, Stephen's logic in responding was convincing. This is clear from the defense he made before the Council. He presented a summary of the Jews' own history and made powerful applications that stung his listeners. During his defense Stephen must have known he was speaking his own death sentence. Members of the Council could not stand to have their evil motives exposed. They stoned him to death while he prayed for their forgiveness. His final words show how much like Jesus he had become in a short time. His death had a lasting impact on young Saul (Paul) of Tarsus, who would move from being a violent persecutor of Christians to being one of the greatest champions of the Gospel the church has known.

Stephen's life is a continual challenge to all Christians. Because he was the first to die for the faith, his sacrifice raises questions. How many risks do we take in being Jesus' followers? Would we be willing to die for him? Are we really willing to live for him? Stephen was stoned, calling upon God, saying, Lord Jesus receive my spirit. And he kneeled down, and cried with a loud voice, Lord lay, not this sin to their charge. And when he had said this, he fell asleep" (Acts 7:59,60).

Stephen saw the glory of God and Jesus the Messiah standing at God's right hand. Stephen's words are similar to Jesus' words spoken before the Council. Stephen's vision supported Jesus' claim and angered the Jewish leaders who had condemned Jesus to death for blasphemy. They would not tolerate Stephen's words, so they dragged him out and killed him. People may not kill us for witnessing about Christ, but they may let us know they don't want to hear the truth and try to silence you. Keep honoring God in your conduct and words; though many may turn against you and your message some will follow Christ. Remember, Stephen's death had a profound impact on Paul, who later became the world's greatest missionary. Even those who oppose us now may later turn to Christ.

Sometime we suffer because of the, I knew-you-when people the result of another's decision and not for any wrong we have done. If you are suffering from unfair rejection, don't blame others and become discouraged. Remember how God used Jephthah despite his unjust circumstances, and realize that he is able to use you even if you feel rejected by some.

Jesus was not the first prophet to be rejected in his own county. Jeremiah experienced rejection in his hometown, even by members of his own family. Life was extremely difficult for Jeremiah despite his love for and obedience to God. When he called to God for relief, God's reply in effect was, "If you think this is bad, how, are you going to cope when it really gets tough?" Not all of God's answers to prayer are nice or easy to cope with. Any Christian who has experienced war, bereavement, or a serious illness knows this. But we are to be committed to God even when the going gets tough and when his answers to our prayers don't bring immediate relief.

In trying to reach us with his love, God finally sent his own Son. His perfect life, his worlds, and his sacrifice of love are meant to cause us to listen to Christ and to follow him as Lord. If we ignore God's gracious gift of his Son, we reject God.

Jesus refers to himself as "the stone which the builders rejected." Though rejected by many of his people, he would become the cornerstone of his new building, the church

Jesus saith unto them, Did ye never read in the scriptures, The stone which the builders rejected the same is become the head of the corner: this is the Lord's doing, and it is marvelous in our eyes. (Matt. 22:42)?

Many people will die in their sins if they reject Christ, because they are rejecting the only way to be rescued from sin. Sadly, many are so taken up with the values of this world that they are blind to the priceless gift Christ offers. Where are you looking? Don't focus on this world's values and miss what is most valuable—eternal life with God.

We may sometimes be afraid to share our faith in Christ because people might feel uncomfortable or reject us. If your courage to witness for God has weakened, pray that your boldness may increase. Remember Jesus' promise, "Whosoever therefore shall confess me before men, him will I confess also before my father which is in heaven."

When we pray, First we praised God; then we tell God our specific problem and asked for his help. We do not ask God to remove our problems but to help us deal with it. We can follow this model when we pray. We may ask God to remove our problems, and he may choose to do so. But we must recognize that often he will leave a problem in place but give us the strength and courage to deal with it.

Have you ever thought of persecution as a blessing? This beating suffered by Peter and John was the first time any of the apostles had been physically abused for their faith. These men knew how Jesus had suffered, and they praised God that he allowed them to be persecuted like their Lord. If you are mocked or persecuted for your faith, it isn't because you're doing something wrong but that God has counted you "worthy to suffer shame for his name."

And they departed from the presence of the council, rejoicing that they were counted worthy to suffer shame for his name (Acts

5:41). Jesus himself was not accepted as a prophet in his hometown. Many people have a similar attitude. Don't be surprised if your Christian life and faith are not easily understood or accepted by those who know you well. Because they know your background, your failures, and your foibles, they may not see past those to the new person you have become. Let God work in your life, pray, to be a positive witness for him, and be patient.

When caught in the storms of life, it is easy to think God has lost control and we're at the mercy of the winds of fate. In reality, God is sovereign. He controls the history of the world and our personal destinies. Just as Jesus calmed the waves, he can calm whatever storms you may face.

To take up the cross meant to carry one's own cross to the place of crucifixion. Many Galileans had been killed that way by the Romans-and Jesus would face it as well. With this word picture, Christ presented a clear and challenging description of the Christian life. Being his disciple means putting aside selfish desires, taking up one's "cross" every day, and following him. It is simple and yet so demanding. For the original Twelve, this meant literal suffering and death. For believers today, it means understanding that we belong to him and that we live to serve his purposes. Consider this: Do you think of your relationship with God primarily in terms of what's in it for you (which is considerable) or in terms of what you can do for him? Are you willing to deny yourself, take up your cross daily, and follow him? Anything less is not discipleship; it is merely superficial lip service.

If this present life is most important to you, you will do everything you can to protect it. You will not want to do anything that might endanger your safety, health, or comfort. By contrast, if following Jesus is most important, you may find yourself in unsafe, unhealthy, and uncomfortable places. You will risk death, but you will not fear it because you know Jesus will raise you to eternal life. Nothing material can compensate for the loss of eternal life. Jesus' disciples are not to use their lives on earth merely to please themselves; they are to spend them serving God and others.

Jesus said he was sending his disciples out "as lambs among wolves." They would have to be careful, for they would surely meet with opposition. We, too, are sent into the world as lambs among wolves. Be alert, and remember to face your enemies, not with aggression, but with love and gentleness. A dangerous mission requires sincere commitment.

The Battle

In the Christian life we battle against "principalities and powers" (the powerful Evil forces of fallen angels headed by Satan, who is a vicious fighter). To withstand their attacks, we must depend on God's strength and use every piece of his armor. Paul is not only giving this counsel to the church, the body of Christ, but to all individuals within the church. The whole body needs to be armed. As you do battle against "the rulers of the darkness of this world," fight in the strength of the church, whose power comes from the Holy Spirit.

> *Be sober, be vigilant; because your adversary the devil, as a roaring lion, walketh about, seeking whom he may devour (1 Peter 5:8).*

Lions attack sick, young or straggling animals; they choose victims who are alone or not alert. Peter warns us to watch out for Satan when we are suffering or persecuted. If you are feeling along, weak, helpless, and cut off from other believers, or if you are so focused on your troubles that you forget to watch for danger, those are the times when you are especially vulnerable to Satan's attacks. During times of suffering, seek other Christians for support. Keep your eyes on Christ and resist the devil. Then, "he will flee from you."

These who are not "flesh and blood" are demons over whom Satan has control. They are not mere fantasies-they are very real. We face a powerful army whose goal is to defeat Christ's church. When we believe in Christ and join his church, these beings become our enemies, and they try every device to turn us away from Christ and back to sin. Although we are assured of victory, we must engage in the struggle unit Christ comes because Satan is constantly battling against all who are on the Lord's side. We need supernatural power to defeat Satan, and God has provided that in his Holy Spirit within us and his armor surrounding us. If you feel discouraged, remember Jesus' words to Peter. "Upon this rock I will build my church; and the gates of hell shall not prevail against it."

Praying always with all prayer and supplication in the Spirit, and watching thereunto with *all perseverance and supplication for all saints (Ephesians 6:18).*

You may ask how anyone can pray all the time. One way to pray constantly is to make quick, brief prayers your habitual response to every situation you meet with throughout the day. Another way is to order your life around God's desires and teachings so that your very life becomes a prayer. You don't have to isolate yourself from other people and from daily work in order to pray constantly. You can make prayer your life and your life a prayer while living in a world that needs God's powerful influence.

I am not praying that God will move my stumbling blocks, but that I will continue to speak boldly for Christ in spite of what some people think. God can use us in any circumstance to do his will. Even as we pray for a change in our circumstances, we should also pray that God will accomplish his plan through us right where we are. Knowing God's eternal purpose for us helps us through the difficult times.

> *But let us, who are of the day, be sober, putting on the breastplate of faith and love; and for an helmet, the hope of salvation (1 Thess. 5:8).*

As you near the end of a long race, your legs ache, your throat burns, and your whole body cries out for you to stop. This is when friends and fans are most valuable. Their encouragement helps you push through the pain to the finish line. In the same way, Christians are to encourage one another. A word of encouragement offered at the right moment can be the difference between finishing well and collapsing along the way. Look around you. Be sensitive to others' need for encouragement and offer supportive words or actions.

For we wrestle not against flesh and blood, but against principalities, against powers, against the rulers of the darkness of this world, against spiritual wickedness in high places (Ephesians 6:12)

From the above Scripture we see that we are in a war. And its not with one another but with the devil and his demons. Jesus called him the father of lies. He lies to you and me to make us believe bad things about ourselves, about other people and about circumstances that are not true.

He knows what we like and what we don't like. He knows our insecurities, our weaknesses and our fears. He knows what get on our nerves the most. He is willing to invest any amount of time it takes to defeat us. One of the devil's strong points is patience he will wait on you.

…. Not by might, nor by power, but by my spirit, saith the LORD of hosts (Zechariah 4:6).

Though this message was spoken to Zerubbabel, it applies to all believers. Military might, political power, or human strength cannot accomplish the work of God. We can only do His work if we are enabled by the Holy Spirit.

One of your weapons is prayer (asking). You can't overcome your situation by determination alone. You do need to be determined, but determined in the Holy Spirit, not in the effort of your own flesh. The Holy Spirit is your Helper—seek His help. Lean on Him. He is strong and able to hold you up.

> *And let us not be weary in well doing: for in due season we shall reap, if we faint not (Galatians 6:9).*

No matter how bad the condition of your life and your mind, don't give up! Take back all your things the devil has stolen from you. The Apostle Paul is encouraging us to keep on keeping on! Don't be a quitter! Don't have that spirit of giving up. God is looking for people who will go all the way through with Him.

Whatever you may be facing or experiencing right now in your life, I am encouraging you to go through it and not give up! You must remember Jesus did not give up on you. You will not give up on Him. When the battle seems endless and you think you'll never make it, remember that the battle is not yours it is the LORD.

Never say I'm not going to make it; this is too hard. I always fail, it has always been the same, and nothing ever changes. I'm sure other people don't have this much trouble getting their minds renewed. I may as well give up. I'm tired of trying. I pray, but it seems as if God doesn't hear me. He probably doesn't answer my prayers because He is so disappointed in the way I act. Remember, you become what you think. Think discouraging thoughts, and you'll get discouraged. Think condemning thoughts, and you'll come under condemnation. Change your thinking and be set free!

AGAINST THE WILES OF THE DEVIL. The Christian is engaged in a spiritual conflict with evil. This spiritual conflict is described as warfare of faith that continues until he enters the life to come. (1) The believer's victory has been secured by Christ Himself through His death on the cross. Jesus waged a triumphant battle against Satan, disarmed the evil powers and authorities of wickedness, led captive a host of captives, and redeemed the believer from Satan's dominion. (2) At the present time Christians are involved in a spiritual warfare that they wage by the power of the Holy Spirit: (a) against the corrupt desires within themselves, (b) against the ungodly pleasures of the world and temptations of every sort, (c) against Satan and his forces. Believers are called upon to separate themselves from the present world system, overcoming and dying to its temptations, and condemning openly its sin. (3) Christian soldiers must wage war against all evil, not in their own power, but with spiritual weapons. (4) In their warfare of faith Christians are called upon to endure hardships as good soldiers of Christ, suffer for the gospel, fight the good fight of faith, wage war, persevere, conquer, be victorious, triumph, defend the gospel, strive for the faith, not be alarmed by opponents, put on the full armor of God, stand form, destroy Satan's strongholds, take captive every thought, become mighty in, and contend for the faith **AGAINST**

PRINCIPALITIES.... POWERS... RULERS. The Christian faces a spiritual conflict with Satan and a host of evil spirits. (1) These powers of darkness are the spiritual rulers of the world who energize the ungodly, oppose God's will, and frequently attack the believers of this age. (2) They constitute a vast multitude and are organized into a highly systematized empire of evil with rank and order.

THE SWORD OF THE SPIRIT. The "sword of the Spirit, which is the word of God," is the believer's offensive weapon to be used in his war against the power of evil. For this reason Satan will make every effort to undermine or destroy the Christian's confidence in that Word. The church must defend the inspired Scriptures against allegations that it is not God's Word in everything it teaches. To abandon the position and attitude of Christ and the apostles toward God's inspired Word is to destroy its power to convict or correct to redeem, to heal, to drive out demons, and to overcome all evil.

Wherefore seeing we also are compassed about with so great a cloud of witnesses, let us lay aside every weight, and the sin which doth so easily beset us, and let us run with patience the race that is set before us (Hebrews 12:1).

What is Paul saying? We do not struggle alone, and we are not the first to struggle with the problems we face. Others have run the race and won, and their witness stirs us to run and win also. Long-distance runners work hard to build endurance and strength. On race day, their clothes are lightweight and their bodies lean. To run the race that God has set before us, we must also lay aside the excess weight that slows us down. How can we do that? (1) Choose friends who are also committed to the race. Wrong friends will have values and activities that may deter you from the course. Much of your own weight may result from the crowd you run with. Make wise choices. (2) Drop certain activities. That is, for you at this time these may be weight. Try dropping them for a while; then check the results in your life. (3) Get help for addictions that disable you. If you have a secret "weight" such as pornography, gambling, or alcohol, admit your need and get help today.

The Christian life involves hard work. It requires us to give up whatever endangers our relationship with God, to run with endurance, and to struggle against sin with the power of the Holy Spirit. To live effectively, we must keep our eyes on Jesus. We stumble when we look away from him to stare at ourselves or at the circumstances surrounding us. We are running for Christ, not ourselves, and we must always keep him in sight.

I have learned through this battle that the race is not given to the swift, nor the battle to the strong, but to the ones that hold out and endure to the end. Jesus took me and made me a fisher of men and women just like he did Peter and Andrew.

These men already knew Jesus. He had talked to Peter and Andrew previously and had been preaching in the area. When Jesus called them, they knew what kind of man he was and were willing to follow him. Jesus told Peter and Andrew to leave their fishing business and become "fishers of men," to help other find God. Jesus was calling them away from their productive trade to be productive spiritually. We all need to fish for souls. If we practice Christ's teachings and share the Gospel with others, we will be able to draw those around us to Christ like a fisherman who pulls fish into his boat with nets.

James and his brother, John, along with Peter and Andrew, were the first disciples Jesus called to work with him. Jesus call motivated these men to get up and leave their jobs—immediately. They didn't make excuses about why it wasn't a good time. They left at once and followed. Jesus calls each of us to follow him. When Jesus asks us to serve him, we must be like the disciples and do it at once.

Jesus preached the Gospel-the Good News-to everyone who wanted to hear it. The Gospel is that the kingdom of heaven has come, that God is with us, and that he cares for us. Christ can heal us, not just of physical sickness, but of spiritual sickness as well. There's no sin or problem too great or too small for him to handle. Jesus' words were good news because they offered freedom, hope, peace, and eternal life with God.

Peter's mother-in-law gives us a beautiful example to follow. He response to Jesus' touch was to "[minister] unto them"—that is, to serve Jesus and his disciples-immediately. Has God ever helped you, through a dangerous or difficult situation? If so, you should ask,

"How can I express my gratitude to him? Because God has promised us all the rewards of his Kingdom, we should look for ways to serve him and his followers now.

Following Jesus is not always easy or comfortable. Often it means great cost and sacrifice, with no earthly rewards or security. Jesus didn't have a place to call home. You may find that following Christ costs you popularity, friendships, leisure time, or treasured habits. But while the cost of following Christ is high, the value of being Christ's disciple is even higher. Discipleship is an investment that lasts for eternity and yields incredible rewards.

When Jesus called Matthew to be one of his disciples, Matthew jumped up and followed, leaving a lucrative career. When God calls you to follow or obey him, do you do it with as much abandon as Matthew? Sometimes the decision to follow Christ requires difficult or painful choices. Like Matthew, we must decide to leave behind those things that would keep us from following Christ.

Jesus gave the disciples a principle to guide their actions as they ministered to others. "Freely ye have received, freely give." Because God has showered us with his blessings, we should give generously to others of our time, love, and possessions.

Jesus said that God is aware of everything that happens even to sparrows, and you are far more valuable to him than they are. You are so valuable that God sent his only Son to die for you. Because God places such value on you, you need never fear personal threats or difficult trials. Theses can't shake God's love or dislodge his Spirit from within you. This doesn't mean, however, that God will take away all your troubles. The real test of value is how well something holds up under the ware, tear, and abuse of everyday life. Those who stand up for God in spite of their troubles truly have lasting value and will receive great rewards.

We cannot imagine all that God has in store for us, both in this life and for eternity. He will create a new heaven and a new earth, and we will live with him forever. Until then, his Holy Spirit comforts and guides us. Knowing the wonderful and future that awaits us gives us hope and courage to press on in this life, to endure hardship, and to avoid in to temptation. This world is not all there is. The best is yet to come.

God's work involves many different individuals with a variety of gifts and abilities. There are no superstars in this task, only team members performing their own special roles. We become useful members of God's team by setting aside our desires to receive glory for what we do. Don't seek the praise that comes from people, because it is comparatively worthless; instead, seek the approval that comes from God.

It is tempting to judge a fellow Christian, evaluating whether or not he or she is a good follower of Christ. But only God knows a person's heart, and he is the only one with the right to judge. When you judge someone, you invariably consider yourself better, and this is pride. Some people talk a lot about faith, but that's all it is talk. They may know all the right words to say, but their lives don't reflect God's power. Paul says the kingdom of God is to be lived, not just discussed. There is a big difference between knowing the right words and living them out. Don't be content to have the right answers about Christ. Let your life show that God's power is really working in you.

Love is more important than knowledge makes us look good and feel important, but one can easily develop an arrogant, know-it-all attitude. Many people with strong opinions are unwilling to listen and learn from God and others. We can obtain God's knowledge only by loving him.

When believers lose the motivation of love, we become critical of others. We stop looking for good in them and see only their faults. Soon we lose our unity. Have you talked behind someone's back? Have you focused on others' shortcoming instead of their strengths? Remind yourself of Jesus' command to love others as we love ourselves. When you begin to feel critical of someone, make a list of that person's positive qualities. When problems need to be addressed, confront in love rather than gossip.

No one should ever think he or she is totally independent and doesn't need help from others, and no one should feel excused from the task of helping others. The body of Christ the universal church-functions only when the members work together for the common good. Is there someone near you who needs help in a task of daily living? Is there a Christian brother or sister who needs correction or encouragement? Humbly and gently reach out to that person and offer to lift his or her load. When you do your very best, you feel good about the results. There is no need to compare you with others. People make comparison for many reasons. Some point out others' flaws in order to feel better about them. Others simply want reassurance that they are doing well. When you are tempted to compare, look at Jesus Christ. His example will inspire you to do your very best, and his loving acceptance will comfort you when you fall short of your goals.

I have been preaching the word of God for seventeen years, I am not tried yet, I been through many trials. I promise the Lord that I will live for him and do for him. I am not struggling alone; I am not the first to struggle with the problems I face. Others have run the race and won, and their witness stirs me to run and win. I run the race that God has set before me; I must lay aside the excess weight that slows me down. How can I do that? (1) I choose friends who are committed to the race. Wrong friends will have values and activities that may deter you from the course. Much of your own weight may result from the crowd you run with. I had to learn that the Christian life involves hard work. It requires us to give up whatever endangers our relationship with God, to run with endurance, and to struggle against sin with the power of the Holy Spirit. To live effectively, we must keep our eyes on Jesus. We stumble when we look away from him to stare at ourselves or at the circumstances surrounding us. We are running for Christ, not for man, not for woman, not for ourselves, and we must always keep him in sight.

People have tried all kinds of ways to please God, but God has made his wishes clear. He wants his people to be fair, just, and merciful, and to walk humbly with him. In your efforts to please God, examine these areas on a regular basis. Are you fair in your dealings with people? Do you show mercy to those who wrong you? Are you learning humility?

I had to learn from experience what it meant to wait on the Lord. I though because God had called me to preach, I could go on and do what I wanted to do. I had to wait on God for the fulfillment of his promise to reign. Waiting on God is not easy. Often it seems that he isn't answering our prayers or doesn't understand the urgency of our situation. That kind of thinking implies that God is not in control or is not fair. But God is worth waiting for. God calls us to wait because often he uses times of waiting to refresh, renew, and teach us. Make good use of your waiting times by discovering what God may be trying to teach you in them.

We often wish we could escape troubles-the pain of grief, loss, sorrow, and failure; or even the small daily frustrations that constantly wear us down. God promises to be our source of power, courage, and wisdom, helping us through our problems. Sometime when we have to wait on God all kinds of trouble come to us. When trouble strikes, don't get frustrated with God. Instead, humbly admit that you need God's help and thank him for being by your side.

Life is short no matter how long we live. If we have something important we want to do, we must not put it off for a better day. Ask yourself, "If I had six months to live, what would I do?" Tell someone that you love him or her? Deal with an undisciplined area in your life? Tell someone about Jesus? Since life is short, don't neglect what is truly important.

I waited patiently for the LORD; and he inclined unto me, and heard my cry. He brought me up also out of an horrible pit, out of the miry clay, and set my feet upon a rock, and established my goings. And he hath a new song in my mouth, even praise unto our God: many shall see it, and fear, and shall trust in the LORD (Psalm 40:1-3).

Waiting for God to help us is not easy, but David received four benefits from waiting: (1) God lifted him out of his despair, (2) God set his feet on firm ground (3) God established his goings (steadied him as he walked), and (4) God gave him a new song. I learned that blessings cannot be received unless we go through the trial of waiting. For some believers, patient waiting becomes the most difficult testing they must face: waiting for illness to pass, for a child to return to God and the church, or for God to make matters right in a particular situation. Are you willing to accepting the Lord's timing, and not

THE BATTLE

your? God alone knows our future. Only God is eternal, and we can trust him to guide us.

(1) This race must be run with "patience," with perseverance and endurance. (2) The race must be run by laying aside the sins that impede or slow us down and by fixing our eyes, lives, and hearts on Jesus and the example of persevering obedience He set on earth. (3) The race must be run with an awareness that the greatest peril confronting us is the temptation to yield to sin, to return to "that country from whence we came out and to become once more citizens of the world. In our race of faith we look to Jesus as (1) our example of trust in God, of commitment to His will of prayer of overcoming temptation and suffering, of endurance in loyalty to the Father, and of seeking the joy of completing the work to which God has called us. (2) our source of strength, love, grace, mercy, and help.

And ye have forgotten the exhortation which speaketh unto you as unto children, My son, despise not thou the chastening of the Lord, nor faint when thou art rebuked of him(Hebrews 12:5).

I learned from that God discipline his children and the hardships and troubles He allows us to suffer. (1) They are a sign that we are children of God. (2) They are an assurance of God's love and concern for us. (3) The Lord's discipline has two purposes: (a) that we might not be finally condemned with the world, and (b) that we might share God's holiness and continue to live sanctified lives without which we will never see the Lord. (4) There are two possible consequences of the Lord's discipline. (a) We may endure the hardships God leads us through, submit to God's will, and continue to remain faithful. By doing this we will continue to live as God's spiritual children and to share His holiness; it will yield the fruit of righteousness. (b) We may "despise" the discipline of our Father, rebel against God because of suffering and hardship, and thereby fall away from God. (5) Under God's will, adversity may come (a) as a result of our spiritual warfare with Satan, (b) as a test to strengthen our faith and our works, or (c) as a preparation for us to comfort others. (6) In all kinds of adversity we must seek God, examine our lives, and forsake all that is contrary to His holiness. Someone may ask what Holiness is. Holiness is being separated from sin and being set apart for God.

It is being close to God, be like Him, and seeking His presence, righteousness, and fellowship with all our hearts. Above all things, holiness is God's priority for His followers. (1) Holiness was God's purpose for His people when He planned their salvation in Christ. (2) Holiness was Christ's purpose for His people when He came to this earth (3) Holiness was Christ's purpose for His people when He gave Himself up for them on the cross. (4) Holiness is God's purpose in making us a new creation and in giving us the Holy Spirit. (5) Without holiness no one can be useful to God. (6) Without holiness there is no nearness to or fellowship with God. (7) Without holiness no one will see the Lord.

No matter how limited our earthly possessions may be or how trying our circumstances, we never need fear that God will desert or forsake us. Scripture declares that the heavenly Father cares for us. "The Lord is my helper, and I will not fear." This can be affirmed with confidence in times of wait, distress, trials, or trouble.

At times, God must discipline us to help us. This is similar to a loving parent disciplining his child. The discipline is not very enjoyable to the child, but is essential to teach him or her right from wrong. The Bible says that "no chastening for the present seemeth to be joyous, but grievous: nevertheless afterward it yieldeth the peaceable fruit of righteousness." When you feel God's hand of correction, accept it as proof of his love. Realize that God is urging you to follow his path instead of stubbornly going your own way. If we believe God is great, we cannot help telling others about him. The best witnessing happens when out hearts are full of appreciation for what he has done. God has chosen to use us to "declare... his wonders among all people." Praise for our great God overflows from his creation and should overflow from our lips. How well are you doing at telling other about God's greatness?

It is a blessing to be disciplined by God when we are wrong. We sometimes give people excellent advice only to learn that it does not apply to them and is therefore not very helpful. All who offer counsel from God's Word should take care to thoroughly understand a person's situation before giving advice. I learned that pain can help us grow. These are good words to remember when we face hardship and loss. Let us all learn from Job, he did not understand why he suffered, his faith in God had a chance to grow. God does not eliminate all hardship when we are following him closely, and good behavior is not always rewarded by prosperity. Rewards for good and punishment for evil are in God's hands and are given out according to his timetable. Satan's ploy is to get us to doubt God's love and faithfulness toward us.

When we are going through severe trials, ill-advised counsel is distasteful. The may listen politely, but inside they are upset. Be slow to give advice to those who are hurting. They often need compassion more than they need advice.

Just like Job, in his grief he wanted to give in, to be freed from his discomfort, and to die. But God did not grant Job's request. He had a greater plan for him. Our tendency, like Job's, is to want to give up and get out when the going gets rough. To trust God in the good times is commendable, but to trust him during the difficult times tests us to our limits and exercises our faith. In your struggles, large or small, trust that God is in control. (Romans 8:28) In his mercy and grace, he will take care of you. Troubles, like "many waters," can threaten to drown us when we are helpless, and weak. How often we wish God would quickly rescue us out of our troubles. Remember that God can either deliver us or help us remain steady as we go through troubles. When you feel as though you are drowning in troubles, ask God to help you, hold you steady, and protect you. In his care, you are never helpless.

Some people think that belief in God is a crutch for weak people who cannot make it on their own. God is indeed a buckler shield to protect us when we are too weak to face certain trials by ourselves, but he does not want us to remain weak. He strengthens, protects, and guides us in order to send us back into an evil world to fight for him. Then he continues to work with us, because the strongest person on earth is infinitely weaker than God and needs his help.

God doesn't promise to eliminate challenges; instead, he promises to give us strength to meet those challenges. If he gave us no rough roads to walk, no mountains to climb, and no battles to fight, we would not grow. He does not leave us alone with our challenges, however. Instead he stands beside us, teaches us, and strengthens us to face them.

Seem like so many times life's problems always seem to go from bad to worse. God is the only one who can reverse this downward spiral. He can take our problems and turn them into glorious victories. The first and most important step is that we must cry out, "Turn thee unto me, and have mercy upon me." When we are willing to do that, God will do his work in us and in our situation. The next step is your, for God has already made his offer.

We often run to God when we experience difficulties. But we should seek God's guiding presence every day. When troubles come our way, we should already be in God's presence and prepared to handle any test. Believers can call to God for help at any time, but how shortsighted to call on God only when troubles come. Many of our problems could be avoided or handled far more easily by seeking God's help and direction beforehand. Many have had the sad experience of being forsaken by father or mother. Broken homes, differences of belief, addiction to drugs or alcohol, even psychological isolation can leave children crippled by this loss. Even as adults, the pain may linger. God can take that place in our life, fill that void, and heal that hurt. He can direct us to those who may take the role of father or mother for us. His love is sufficient for all our needs.

So many times when we are experience problem after problem waiting on God is not easy. Often it seems that he isn't answering our prayers or doesn't understand the urgency of our situation. That kind of thinking implies that God is not in control or is not fair. But God is worth waiting for [Isaiah 40:27-31].

God uses times of waiting to refresh, renew, and teach us. Make good use of your waiting times by discovering what God may be trying to teach you in them.

The kind of prayer that moves mountains is prayer for the fruitfulness of God's Kingdom. It would seem impossible to move a mountain into the sea, so Jesus used that picture to show that God can do anything. God will answer your prayers, but not as a result of your positive mental attitude. Other conditions must be met: (1) You must be a believer; (2) you must not hold a grudge against another person; (3) you must not pray with selfish motives; (4) your request must be for the good of his Kingdom. To pray effectively, you need faith in God, not faith in the object of your request. If you focus only on your request, you will be left with nothing if your request is refused.

Jesus, our example, once prayed, "All things are possible unto thee;...nevertheless not what I will, but what thou wilt." Our prayers are often motivated by our own interests and desires. We like to hear that we can have anything. But Jesus prayed with God's interests in mind. When we pray, we can express our desires, but we should want his will above ours. Check yourself to see if your prayers focus on your interests or God's.

I have been hurt so many times running this race, I know forgiving others is tough work-so much so that many people would rather do something totally distasteful than offer forgiveness to someone who has wronged them. For a person to pray while bearing a grudge, however, is like a tree sprouting leaves and bearing no fruit. True faith changes the heart. Real faith seeks peace. For our churches to have prayer power there must be harmony and forgiveness evident in the body of believers. Let go of hurts, abandon grudges, and forgive others.

I often think about what life will be like after the resurrection is for beyond our ability to understand or imagine. We need not be afraid of eternal life because of the unknowns, however, Instead of wondering what God's coming Kingdom will be like; we should concentrate on our relationship with Jesus right now, because in the new Kingdom we will be with him. I have learned to love; let go of my hurts, grudges, forgive others and trust Jesus, we will not be afraid of what he has in store for us then.

> *For since the beginning of the world men have not heard, nor perceived by the ear, neither hath the eye seen, O God, beside thee, what he hath prepared for him that waiteth for him [Isaiah 64:4].*

God is merciful even to rebels, if they confess their sins and return to him. Don't let your hurts, grudges, not loving one another keep you from turning to God. He is waiting for you with open arms.

Some think that troubles are always caused by sin or a lack of faith. Troubles may be a part of God's plan for believers. Going through trials can build character, patience, and sensitivity toward others who also face trouble. Problems are unavoidable for God's people. Your troubles may be a sign of effective Christian living.

Some people turn to God hoping to escape suffering on earth. Rather than escape from suffering, God gives us power to grow through our suffering. The Christian life is marked by obedience to Christ despite temptations and hardships.

Sometimes we feel that if the Holy Spirit leads us, it will always be "beside the still waters." But that is not necessarily true. He led Jesus into the wilderness for a long and difficult time of testing, and he may also lead us into difficult situations. When facing trials, first make sure you haven't brought them on yourself through sin or unwise choices. If you find no sin to confess or unwise behavior to change, then ask God to strengthen you for your test. Finally, be careful to follow faithfully wherever the Holy Spirit leads you.

The devil, who tempted Adam and Eve in the garden, also tried to tempt Jesus in the wilderness. Satan is a real being, a created but rebellious fallen angel, not a symbol or an idea. He constantly fights against God and those who follow and obey God. Jesus was a prime target for his temptations. Satan had succeeded with Adam and Eve, and he hope to succeed with Jesus as well.

Knowing and obeying God's Word is an effective weapon against temptation, the only offensive weapon provided in the Christian's "armor" Jesus used Scripture to counter Satan's attacks, and so should we. But to use it effectively, we must have faith in God's promises because Satan also knows Scripture and is adept at twisting it to suit his purpose. Obeying the Scriptures is more important than simply having a verse to quote, so read them daily and apply them to your life. Then your "sword" will always be sharp.

Why was it necessary for Jesus to be tempted? First, temptation is part of the human experience. For Jesus to be fully human, for him to understand us completely, he had to face temptation. Second, Jesus had to undo Adam's work. Adam, though created perfect, gave in to temptation and passed sin on to the whole human race. Jesus, by contrast, resisted Satan. His victory offers salvation to all of Adam's descendants.

> *And David inquired of God, saying, Shall I go up against the Philistines? And wilt thou deliver them into mine hand? And the LORD said unto him, Go up; for I will deliver them into thine hand [1 Chronicles 14:10].*

Before David went to battle, he talked to God, asking for his presence and guidance. Too often we wait until we are in trouble before turning to God. By the consequences of our actions are already unfolding. When do you ask God's help, only as a desperate last resort? Instead, go to him first! Like David, you may receive incredible help and avoid serious trouble. Make sure you give God the credit when you see what he does on your behalf.

> *And they went up on the breadth of the earth, and compassed the camp of the saints about, and the beloved city: and fire came down from God out of heaven, and devoured them [Rev. 20:9].*

This is not a typical battle where the outcome is in doubt during the heat of the conflict. Here there is no contest. Two mighty forces of evil-those of the beast and of Satan unite to do battle against God. The Bible uses just two verses to describe each battle-the evil beast and his forces are captured and thrown into the lake of fire, and fire from God consumes Satan and his attacking armies. For God, it is as easy as that. There will be no doubt, no worry, no second thoughts for believers about whether they have chosen the right side. If you are with God, you will experience this tremendous victory with Christ.

I Will Bless The Lord At All Times

> *I will bless the LORD at all times: his praise shall continually be in my mouth [Psalm 34:1].*

God promises great blessings to his people, but many of these blessings require active participation. He will free us from fear, deliver us from trouble, guard us, show us kindness, supply our needs, listen when we talk to him, and redeem us, but we must do our part. We can appropriate his blessings when we seek him, cry out to him, trust him, fear him, keep from lying, turn from sin, do good, and seek peace, have humble hearts, and serve him. When you are in trouble, do you feel discouraged and defeated? David did. He kept running, and running, and running, it looked like it would never come to an end. He lost heart and was discouraged. He thought, one of these days he would be killed. Yet he says, "I will bless the LORD at all times." I do pretty well in praising the Lord on a good sunshiny day and when things go right, but it is not so easy when things become difficult. Yet David could say, "His praise shall continually be in my mouth".

> *O taste and see that the LORD is good: blessed is the man that trusteth in him [Psalm 34:8]*

"Taste and see" does not mean, "Check out God's credentials." Instead, it is a warm invitation: "Try this; I know you'll like it." When we take that first step of obedience in following God, we will discover that he is good and kind. When we begin the Christian life, our knowledge of God is partial and incomplete. As we trust him daily, we experience how good he is. David says, "If you don't believe what I have said is true, taste for yourself and see that the Lord is good." Blessed or *happy* is the man who trusts in the Lord. There is nothing like it.

> [*Matt. 11:28: Come unto me, all ye that labour and are heavy-laden and I will give you rest. 29vs. Take my yoke upon you, and learn of me; for I am meek and lowly in heart: and ye shall find rest unto your souls. 30vs. For my yoke is easy, and my burden is light.*]

When you feel down, you may find it difficult to give thanks. Take heart-God works all things out for good if we love him and are fitting into his plans. Thank God, not for your problems but for the strength he is building in you through the difficult experiences of your life. You can be sure that God's perfect love will see you through.

I have learned in my walk with Jesus he works out all things-not just isolated incidents-for our good. This does not mean that all that happens to us is good. Because evil is prevalent in our fallen world, but God is able to turn it around for our long-range good. God is not working to make us happy but to fulfill his purpose. Also, this promise is not for everybody. It can be claimed only by those who love God and are fitting into God's plans. Those who are "called," and those that the Holy Spirit convinces, will receive Christ.

Through all my trials and tribulations God stayed by my side he did not leave me. I will bless the Lord at all times. The writer of this psalm praises the Lord for a miraculous deliverance from great trouble. My testimony encourages all afflicted believers to believe that they may also experience the goodness of the Lord.

Remember, God knows what we need, and our deepest needs are spiritual. Even though many Christians face unbearable poverty and hardship, they still have enough spiritual nourishment to live for God. To have God is to have all you really need. God is enough. If you feel you don't have everything you need, ask: (1) Is this really a need? (2) Is this really good for me? (3) Is this the best time for me to have what I desire? Even if you answer yes to all three questions, God may allow you to go without, to help you grow more dependent on him. He may want you to learn that you need him more than having your immediate desires met.

> *Come, ye children, hearken unto me: I will teach you the fear of the LORD [Psalm 34:11].*

The Bible often connects the fear of the Lord (love and reverence for him) with obedience. "Fear God, and keep his commandments;" If a man love me, he will keep my words. Those who truly love Jesus and obey His words will experience the immediate presence and love of the Father and the Son. The Father and the Son come to believers by means of the Holy Spirit. David said that a person who fears the Lord doesn't lie, turns from sin, does well, and promotes peace. Reverence is much more than sitting quietly in church. It includes obeying God in the way we speak and the way we treat others.

Some may think that peace should come with no effort. But David explained that we are to seek and pursue peace. Paul echoed this thought in Romans 12:18. A person who wants peace cannot be argumentative and contentious. Since peaceful relationships come from our efforts at peacemaking, work hard at living in peace with others each day. If we love someone the way Christ loves us, we will be willing to forgive. If we have experienced God's grace, we will want to pass it on to others. And remember, grace is undeserved favor. By giving an enemy a drink, we're not excusing his misdeeds. We're recognizing him, forgiving him, and loving him in spite of his sins-just as Christ did for us.

Jesus said to rejoice when we're persecuted. Persecution can be good because (1) it takes our eyes off earthly rewards, (2) it strips away superficial belief, (3) it strengthens the faith of those who endure, and (4) our attitude through it serves as an example to others who follow. We can be comforted to know that God's greatest prophets were persecuted. Our persecution means we have shown ourselves faithful. In the future, God will reward the faithful by letting them enter his eternal Kingdom, where there is no more persecution.

So many times when we are going through trials, we will say Lord why me, then I think why not me. Through my trials I will bless the Lord at all times, His praise shall continually be in my mouth. If you are waiting for the sun shine in your life, or for it to be a sunny day before you praise the Lord, you might never praise him. We have to learn how to praise our way out of darkness and stop complaining and feeling sorry for ourselves. David did not complain going through his trials, He said I will bless the Lord at all times.

God promises great blessings to his people, but these blessings require active participation, he will free us from fear, deliver us from trouble, guard us, show us kindness, supply our needs, listen when we talk to him, and redeem us. But we must do our part. David said I will bless the Lord at all times no matter what we are going through.

> *These things I have spoken unto you, that in me ye might have peace. In the world ye shall have tribulation: but be of good cheer; I have overcome the world [John 16:33].*

I have learned through my trials that Jesus wants us to take courage. In spite of the inevitable struggles we will face, we are not alone. Jesus does not abandon us in our struggles either. If we remember that the ultimate victory has already been won, we can claim the peace of Christ in the most troublesome times. So many times Jesus will take us through the process just to see how well we are living out what we say we believe about him.

> *But I say unto you Love your enemies, bless them that curse you, do good to them that hate you, and pray for them which despitefully use you, and persecute you [Matt.6:44].*

By telling us not to retaliate, Jesus keeps us from taking the law into our own hands. By loving and praying for our enemies, we can overcome evil with good. The Pharisees interpreted Leviticus 19:18 teachings that they should love only those who love in return. And they thought that meant they should hate their enemies. But Jesus says we are to love our enemies. If you love your enemies and treat them well, you will truly show that Jesus is Lord of your life. This is possible only for those who give themselves fully to God, because only he can deliver people from natural selfishness. We must trust the Holy Spirit to help us show love to those for whom we may not feel love.

My father and mother taught us how to love, they always told us to love everybody even our enemies, even the ones that have hurt us. We hurt Jesus but he still Love us. Sincere love involves selfless giving a self-centered person can't truly love. God's love and forgiveness will free you and take your eyes off yourself to meet others' needs. By sacrificing his life, Christ showed that he truly loves us.

We often run to God when we experience difficulties. But David sought God's guiding presence every day. When troubles came his way, he was already in God's presence and prepared to handle any test. Believers can call to God for help as any time, but how shortsighted to call on God only when troubles come. Many of our problems could be avoided or handled far more easily by seeking God's help and direction beforehand.

Waiting on God is not easy. Often it seems that he isn't answering our prayers or doesn't understand the urgency of our situation. That kind of thinking implies that God is not in control or is not fair. But God is worth waiting for. Isaiah 40:27-31 calls us to wait because often God uses times of waiting to refresh, renew, and teach us. Make good use of your waiting times by discovering what God may be trying to teach you in them.

> *How long wilt thou forget me, O LORD? For ever? How long wilt thou hide they face from me? [Psalms13:1]*

Sometimes all we need to do is talk over a problem with a friend to help put it in perspective. David expressed his feelings to God and found strength. By the end of his prayer, he was able to profess hope and trust in God. Through prayer we can express our feelings and talk our problems out with God. He helps us regain the right perspective, and this gives us peace.

Living for God in a deceitful world can be difficult and lonely. At one time the great prophet felt so lonely he wanted to die. But God told him that there were 7,000 other faithful servants. We are never alone in our battle against evil. When you feel alone, seek out other believers for strength and support.

David said in Psalm 35:13, But as for me, when they were sick, my clothing was sackcloth: I humbled my soul with fasting; and my prayer returned into mine own bosom. So many times you might feel like David. "My prayer returned into mine own bosom" means "my prayer went unanswered." When our deliverance is delayed, we may assume God hasn't answered our prayer. God hears every prayer, but he answers according to his wisdom. Don't let the absence of an immediate answer cause you to doubt or resent God. Instead let it be an occasion to deepen your faith.

David cried out to God to defend him when people wrongly accused him. If you are unjustly accused, your natural reaction may be to lash out in revenge or to give a detailed defense of your move. Ask God to fight the battle for you.

We may believe that God wants to hear only certain requests from us. While it is true that we should offer praise, confession, and respectful petitions, I learned that it is true that God is willing to listen to anything we want to tell him. God will always listen attentively and will fully understand us.

If we believe God is great, we cannot help telling others about him. The witnessing happens when our hearts are full of appreciation for what he has done. God has chosen to use us to "declare... His wonders among all people." Praise for our great God overflows from his creation and should overflow from our lips. How well are you doing at telling others about God's greatness?

David tells us to acknowledge that the Lord is God! How can we do that? We acknowledge him when we shout our praises, appreciate his status as our Creator, accept his authority in every detail of life, enthusiastically agree with the guidance he gives us, and express our thanks for his unfailing love.

God alone is worthy of being worshiped. What is your attitude toward worship? Do you willingly and joyfully come into God's presence, or are you just going through the motions, reluctantly going to church? Remember God's goodness and dependability, and then to worship with thanksgiving and praise.

> *Bless the LORD, O my soul: and all that is within me, bless his holy name [Psalm 103:1]*

David's praise focused on the good things God was doing for him. It is easy to complain about life, but David's list gives us plenty for which to praise God-his forgiveness, healing, redemption, lovingkindness, tender mercies, providence, righteousness, justice, grace, patience. We receive all of these without deserving any of them. No matter how difficult your life's journey, you can always count your blessings-past, present, and future. When you feel as if you have nothing for which to praise God, take time out and read David's list.

If God seems far away, persist in your search for him. God reward those who sincerely look for him. Jesus promised, "Seek, and ye shall find." How do you search for him? Study your Bible; you will discover a loving God who is waiting for us to find him.

> *O give thanks unto the LORD; for he is good: because his mercy endureth for ever [Psalm 118:1]*

Have you ever said, "I can't think of anything God has done for me? How can I praise him?" This psalm gives two reasons for praising God: He is merciful, and his truth endures forever. If He did nothing else for us our whole lives, He would still be worthy of our highest praise.

Sometimes we feel as if we don't understand ourselves what we want, how we feel, what's wrong with us, or what we should do about it. But God's understanding is infinite, and therefore he understands us fully. If you feel troubled and don't understand yourself, remember that God understands you perfectly. Take your mind off yourself and focus in on God. Strive to become more and more like him. The more you learn about God and his ways, the better you will understand yourself.

O sing unto the LORD a new song; for he hath done marvelous things: his right hand, and his holy arm, hath gotten him the victory [Psalm 98:1]

This is a psalm of praise anticipating the coming of God to rule the people. Jesus fulfilled this anticipation when he came to save all people from their sins, and he will come again to judge the world. God is both perfectly loving and perfectly just. He is merciful when He punishes, and He overlooks no sin when He loves. Praise Him for His promise to save you and to return again.

PRAYING FOR RESULTS

Prayer is a conversation of the heart with God. Through prayer, we align ourselves with our Creator, and His presence is revealed to us. We grow in love through worshipping Him. In addition, when we are united with our Lord through prayer, our life becomes fuller, richer, more joyous and more peaceful.

Prayer is a cleansing process, washing our thoughts, feelings, motives, and will, purifying the entire being including the heart, thus enabling us to see God, for without purity no one can see God.

In the Lord's Prayer, Jesus invites us to draw near to God who is beyond human understanding, who dwells in mystery, who is all-holy. We can call God "our Father."

By calling God "Father," we are more rightly describing ourselves and our relationship with God. Jesus teaches that we have a filial relationship with God; God sees us as if we were a daughter or a son. In addition, we, on our part, can approach God in the familiar confident way a child approaches a loving parent.

Repeating the same words over and over like a magic incantation is no way to ensure that God will hear our prayer. It's not wrong to come to God many times with the same requests-Jesus encourages *persistent* prayer. But he condemns the shallow repetition of words that are not offered with a sincere heart. We can never pray too much if our prayers are honest and sincere.

After this manner therefore pray ye: Our Father which are in heaven, Hallowed be thy name [Matt. 6:9].

This is often called the Lord's prayers because Christ gave it to the disciples as a model for them (and us) to keep in mind as we pray. Jesus provided a pattern to be imitated as well as duplicated. We should praise God, pray for his work in the world, pray for our daily needs, and pray for help in our daily struggles.

The phrase "Our Father which art in heaven" indicates that God is not only majestic and holy, but also personal and loving. The first line of this model prayer is a statement of praise and a commitment to hallow, or honor, God's holy name. We can honor God's name by being careful to use it respectfully. If we use God's name lightly, we aren't remembering God's holiness.

"Thy kingdom come" is a reference to God's spiritual reign, not Israel's freedom from Rome. God's Kingdom was announced in the covenant with Abraham (Luke 13:28), is present in Christ's reign in believers' hearts (Luke 17:21), and will be complete when all evil is destroyed and God establishes the new heaven and earth (Rev. 21:1).

When we pray "Thy will be done," we are not resigning ourselves to fate but praying that God's perfect purpose will be accomplished in this world as well as in the next. And how does God accomplish his will on earth? He does it largely through people willing to obey him. This part of the prayer allows us to offer ourselves as doers of God's will, asking him to guide, lead, and give us the means to accomplish his purposes.

When we pray "Give us this day our daily bread," we are acknowledging that God is our Sustainer and Provider. It is a misconception to think that we provide for our needs ourselves. We must trust God daily to provide what he knows we need.

God sometimes allows us to be tested by temptation. As disciples, we should pray to be delivered from these trying times and for deliverance from Satan ("evil") and his deceit. All Christians struggle with temptation. Sometimes it is so subtle that we don't even realize what is happening to us. God has promised that He will not allow us to be tempted beyond our endurance. Ask God to help you recognize temptation and to give you strength to overcome it and choose God's way.

Jesus gives a startling warning about forgiveness: If we refuse to forgive others, God will also refuse to forgive us. Why? Because when we don't forgive others, we are denying our common ground as sinners in need of God's forgiveness. God's forgiveness of sin is not the direct result of our forgiving others, but it is based on our realizing what forgiveness means. It is easy to ask God for forgiveness but difficult to grant it to others. Whenever we ask God to forgive us for sin, we should ask ourselves, "Have I forgiven the people who have wronged me?"

Praying morning, noon, and night is certainly an excellent way to maintain correct priorities throughout every day. The prayers of God's people are effective against the overwhelming evil in the world. You may find it difficult to pray for those in authority if they are evil, but that is when your prayers are most needed. When you enter times of trouble or sudden change, pray diligently and move ahead, doing whatever you can rather than giving up because of fear and uncertainty.

> *And it came to pass, that, as he was praying in a certain place, when he ceased, one of his disciples said unto him, Lord, teach us to pray, as John also taught his disciples [Luke 11:1].*

Notice the order in this prayer. First Jesus praise God; then he makes his requests. Praising God first puts us in the right frame of mind to tell him about our needs. Too often our prayers are more like shopping lists than conversations. These verses focus on three aspects of prayer: its content, our persistence, and God's faithfulness.

God's provision is daily, not once and for all. We cannot store it up and then cut off communication with God, and we dare not be self-satisfied. If you are running low on strength, ask your self-how long have I been away from the source?

When Jesus taught his disciples to pray, he made forgiveness the cornerstone of their relationship with God. God has forgiven our sins; we must now forgive those who have wronged us. To remain unforgiving shows we have not understood that we ourselves deeply need to be forgiven. Think of some people who have wronged you.

Have you truly forgiven them? How will God deal with you if he treats you as you treat others?

Persistence in prayer overcomes our insensitivity, not God's. It does more to change our heart and mind than His. It helps us understand and express the intensity of our need. Persistence in prayer helps us recognize God's work when we see it.

What does Jesus want from us? He wants total dedication, not halfhearted commitment. We can't pick and choose among Jesus' ideas and follow him selectively; we have to accept the cross along with the crown. We must count the cost and be willing to abandon everything else that has given us security without looking back. With our focus on Jesus, we should allow nothing to distract us from following him.

> *And he spake a parable unto them to this end, that men ought always to pray, and not to* faint [Luke 18:1].

To persist in prayer until the answer comes does not mean endless repetition or painfully long prayer sessions. Always praying means keeping our requests constantly before God as we live for him day by day, always believing He will answer. When we thus live by faith, we are not to give up. God may delay answering, but His delays always have good reasons. As we persist in prayer we grow in character, faith, and hope.

Reading God's Word any time we have set aside to pray also helps focus that time on God, not on worldly distractions or ourselves. When we study His Word, we put God as our top priority and we want to be united with Him through prayer.

> *Be still before the Lord and wait patiently for him* [Psalm 37:7].

When we are in prayer with God, we need to be focused solely on Him. To "be still" as the psalmist says, is seeking to hear His voice in our life. As we develop a lifestyle of prayer, we strive to focus our thoughts on our Redeemer all the time.

> *And the LORD said, Because the cry of Sodom and Gomorrah is great, and because their sin is very grievous; I will go down now, and see whether they have done altogether according to the cry of it, which is come unto me; and if not, I will know [Genesis 18:20-21].*

Did Abraham change God's mind? No he did not. The more likely answer is that God changed Abraham's mind. Abraham knows God is just and He punishes sin. But he may have wondered about God's mercy. Abraham seemed to be probing God's mind to see how merciful He really is. He left his conversation with God convinced that God was both kind and fair.

Our prayers may not change God's mind, but they may change ours just as Abraham's prayer changed his. Prayer is a means through which we can better comprehend the mind of God.

> *And Isaac intreated the LORD for his wife, because she was barren: and the LORD was intreated of him, and Rebekah his wife conceived [Genesis 25:21].*

As Isaac pleaded with God for children, we must ask and even plead for our most personal and important requests. God wants to give us good things, but He wants us to ask for them. Even then, as Isaac learned, God may decide to withhold His answer for a while in order to (1) deepen our insight into what we really need, (2) broaden our appreciation for his answers, or (3) allow us to mature so we can use his gifts more wisely.

Be careful for nothing; but in every thing by prayer and supplication with thanksgiving let your requests be made known unto God [Philippians 4:6].

"Be careful for nothing" means don't worry. Imagine never worrying about anything! It seems like impossible-we all have worries on the job, in our home, at school. But Paul's advice is to turn your worries into prayers. Do you want to worry less? Then pray more! Whenever you start to worry, stop and pray. God's peace is different from the world's peace. It is not found in positive thinking, in absence of conflict, or in good feelings. Real peace comes from knowing that because God is in control, our citizenship in Christ's Kingdom is sure, our destiny is set, and our victory over sin is certain.

When Joshua first went against Ai, he did not consult God but relied on the strength of his army to defeat the small city. Only after Israel was defeated did they turn to God and ask, "What happened?" Too often we rely on our own skills and strength, especially when the task before us seems easy. We go to God only when the obstacles seem too great. However, only God knows what lies ahead. Consulting Him, even when we are on a winning streak, may save us from grave mistakes or misjudgments. God may want us to learn lessons, remove pride, or consult others before he will work through us. Sometimes people wonder why their prayers are not answered. But if they don't fulfill the responsibilities God has already given them, they should not be surprised when he does not give further guidance.

2 Samuel 7:8-16 David's request was good, but God said "no." This does not mean that God rejected David. In fact, God was planning to do something even greater in David's life than allowing him the prestige of building the temple. Although God turned down David's request, He promised to continue the house of David forever. David's earthly dynasty ended four centuries later, but Jesus Christ, a direct descendant of David, was the ultimate fulfillment of this promise. Christ will reign for eternity-now in his spiritual kingdom and in heaven, and later, on earth, in the New Jerusalem. Have you prayed with good intentions, only to have God say "no"? This is God's way of directing you to a greater purpose in your life. Accepting God's "no" requires as great a faith as carrying out His "yes."

In spite of Samson's past, God still answered his prayer and destroyed the heathen temple and worshipers. God still loved him. He was willing to hear Samson's prayer of confession and repentance and use him this final time. One of the effects of sin in our lives is to keep us from feeling like praying. But perfect moral behavior is not a condition for prayer. Don't let guilt feelings over sin keep you from your only means of restoration. No matter how long you have been away from God, He is ready to hear from you and restore you to a right relationship with Him. Every situation can be salvaged if you are willing to turn again to Him. If God could still work in Samson's situation, He can certainly make something worthwhile out of your life.

> *And she was in bitterness of soul, and prayed unto the LORD, and wept sore [1 Samuel 1:10].*

Many Old Testament leaders (such as Abraham, Jacob, and David) had more than one wife; this was not God's original intention for marriage. Genesis 2:24 states that in marriage, two people become one flesh. Why then did polygamy exist among God's people? First, it was to produce more offsprings to help in the man's work and to assure the continuation of the man's family line. Numerous children were a symbol of status and wealth. Second, in societies many young men were killed in battle, polygamy became an accepted way of supporting women who otherwise would have remained unmarried and, very likely, destitute. Nevertheless, polygamy often caused serious family problems, as we see in the story of Hannah and Peninnah.

Hannah had been unable to conceive children, and in Old Testament times, a childless woman was considered a failure. Her barrenness was a social embarrassment for her husband. Children were a very important part of society's economic structure. They were a source of labor for the family, and it was their duty to care for their parents in their old age. If a wife could not bear children she was often obligated, by ancient Middle Eastern custom, to give one of her servant girls to her husband to bear children for her. Although Elkanah could have left Hannah (a husband was permitted to divorce a barren wife), he remained lovingly devoted to her despite social criticism and his rights under civil law.

Part of God's plan for Hannah involved postponing her years of childbearing. While Peninnah and Elkanah looked at Hannah's outward circumstances, God was moving ahead with his plan. Can you think of others who are struggling with the way God is working in their lives and who need our support? By supporting those who are struggling, you may help them remain obedient to God and confident in his timing to bring fulfillment to their lives.

Hannah knew her husband loved her, but even his encouragement could not comfort her. She could not keep from listening to Peninnah's jeers and letting her words erode her self-confidence. Although we cannot keep others from unjustly criticizing us, we can choose how we react to the criticism. Rather than dwelling on our problems, we can enjoy the loving relationships God has brought into our lives. By so doing, we can exchange self-pity for hope.

Hannah had good reason to feel discouraged. She was unable to bear children; she shared her husband with a woman who ridiculed her; her loving husband could not solve her problem; and even the High Priest misunderstood her motives. But instead of retaliating or giving up hope, Hannah prayed. She brought her problem honestly before God.

Each of us may face times of barrenness in our lives when nothing "comes to birth" in our work, service, or relationships. It is difficult to pray in faith when we feel so ineffective. But prayer opens the way for God to work, as Hannah discovered.

Be careful what you promise in prayer because God may take you up on it. Hannah so desperately wanted her prayer to be answered that she was willing to strike a bargain with God. God took her up on her promise, and to Hannah's credit, she followed through on her part, even though painful.

Although we are not in a position to barter with God, he may still choose to answer a prayer which has an attached promise. When you pray and promises God something, ask yourself, "Will I follow through on any promises I make to God if He grants my request?" It is dishonest and dangerous to ignore a promise, especially to God. God keeps his promises and He expects you to keep yours.

When you notice something is wrong with another person, what is your first reaction? Eli made a snap judgment before he knew all the facts. It is easy to misunderstand motives and actions. Be sensitive to the fact that, like Hannah, someone may be facing tremendous burdens. Before you make a judgment, find out what a person may be going through.

Earlier Hannah had been discouraged to the point of being physically sick and unable to eat. This is the antidote for discouragement. Here she returns home well and happy. The change in her attitude may be attributed to three factors: (1) She honestly prayed to God; (2) she received encouragement from Eli; (3) she resolved to leave the problem with God. Tell God how you really feel and leave your problems with him.

Is failing to pray for others a sin? Samuel's words seem to indicate that it is. His actions illustrate two of God's people's responsibilities: (1) They should pray consistently for others, and (2) they should teach others the right way to God. Samuel disagreed with the Israelites' demand for a king, but he assured them that he would continue to pray for them and teach them. We may disagree with someone, but we shouldn't stop praying for him or her.

> *Moreover as for me, God forbid that I should sin against the LORD in ceasing to pray for you: but I will teach you the good and the right way [1 Samuel 12:23]*

Samuel became irritated with Saul because he was always looking for a military answer to his problems instead of a spiritual one. Saul often performed spiritual functions out of duty rather than from his heart. Be sure your serving is based on the love of God and His people, and not merely out of duty. Samuel was hoping that God would answer his prayers and change Saul.

Samuel reminded the people to take time to recall all the good things God had done for them. Taking time for reflection allows us to focus attention upon God's goodness and strengthens our faith. Sometimes we are so progress-and future-oriented that we fail to take time to consider all that God has already done. Make it a practice to review what God has done for you so that you may move ahead with a grateful attitude.

> *But will God in very deed dwell with men on the earth? Behold, heaven and the heaven of heavens cannot contain thee, how much less this house which*

I have built! Have respect therefore to the prayer of thy servant, and to his supplication, O LORD my God, to hearken unto the cry and the prayer which thy servant prayeth before thee [2 Chronicles 6:18-19]

The Temple was a place where the people could worship God. God did not need a Temple to live in, because not even the highest heaven could contain Him. But at the Temple God was present in a special way among His people. While it is true that we can praise God and pray anywhere anytime, gathering with others for singing and praising enhances our worship. It also strengthens our resolve to follow God. Solomon marveled that the Temple could contain the power of God and that God would be willing to live on earth among sinful people. We marvel that God, through his Son, Jesus, lived among us in human form to reveal His eternal purposes to us. In doing so, God was reaching out to us in love. God wants us to reach out in return and get to know Him. Only then will we come to love Him with all our hearts. Do not simply marvel at His power; take time to get to know Him.

As Solomon led the people in prayer, he asked God to hear prayers concerning a variety of situations: (1) crime; (2) enemy attacks; (3) drought; (4) famine; (5) the influx of foreigners; (6) war; and (7) sin. God is concerned with whatever we face, even the difficult circumstances we bring upon ourselves. He wants us to turn to Him in prayer. Remember when you pray God hears you. Do not let the extremity of your situation cause you to doubt His care for you.

So we fasted and besought our God for this: and he was intreated of us [Ezra 8:23].

Ezra knew God's promises to protect His people, but he didn't take them for granted. He also knew that God's blessings are appropriated through prayer, so Ezra and the people humbled themselves by fasting and prayer. And their prayers were answered. Fasting humbled them because going without food reminded them of their complete dependence on God's provision. Fasting also gave extra time to pray and meditate on God.

Too often we pray glibly and superficially. Serious prayer, by contrast, requires concentration and desire. It puts us in touch with God's will and can really change us. Without serious prayer, we reduce God to a quick-service pharmacist with painkillers for our every ailment.

Sleep does not come easily during a crisis. David could have had sleepless nights when his son Absalom rebelled and gathered an army to kill him. But he slept peacefully, even during the rebellion. What made the difference? David cried out to the Lord, and the Lord heard him. The assurance of answered prayer brings peace. It is easier to sleep well when we accept with full assurance that God is in control of our circumstances. If you are lying awake at night worrying about what you can't change, pour out your heart to God, and thank him that He is in control. Then sleep will come.

> *But know that the LORD hath set apart him that is godly for himself: the LORD will hear when I call unto him [Psalm 4:3].*

The godly are those who are faithful and devoted to God. David knew that God would hear him when he called and would answer him. We, too, can be confident that God listens and answers when we call on him. Sometimes we think God will not hear us because we have fallen short of His high standards for holy living. But God has forgiven us and He will listen to us. When you feel that your prayers are "bouncing off the ceiling," remember that as a believer you have been set apart by God and that He loves you. He hears and answers (although his answers may not be what you expect). Look at your problems in the light of God's power instead of looking at God in the shadow of your problems.

> *Pray for the peace of Jerusalem: they shall prosper that love thee [Psalm 122:6].*

The writer was not praying for his own peace and prosperity, but for that of his fellow citizens in Jerusalem. This is intercessory prayer, prayer on behalf of others. Too often we pray for our own needs and desires when we should be interceding for others. Will you intercede for someone in need today? The peace sought in these verses is much more than the mere absence of conflict. It suggests completeness, health, justice, prosperity, and protection. The world cannot provide this peace. Real peace comes from faith in God because He alone embodies all the characteristics of peace. To find peace of mind and peace with others, you must find peace with God.

> *I thank thee, and praise thee, O thou God of my fathers, who hast given me wisdom and might, and hast made known unto me now what we desired of thee: for thou hast now made known unto us the king's matter [Daniel 2:23].*

After Daniel asked God to reveal Nebuchadnezzar's dream to him, he saw a vision of the dream. His prayer was answered. Before rushing to Arioch with the news, Daniel took time to give God credit for all wisdom and power, thanking Him for answering his request. How do you feel when your prayers are answered? Excited, surprised, relieved? There are times when we seek God in prayer and, after having been answered, dash off in our excitement, forgetting to give God credit for the answer. Match your persistence in prayer with gratitude when your requests are answered.

Although Daniel knew about the law against praying to anyone except the king, he still prayed to God three times a day as he always had. Daniel has a disciplined prayer life. Our prayers are usually interrupted not by threats, but simply by the pressure of our schedules. Do not let threats or pressures cut into your prayer time. Pray regularly, no matter what.

> *Then Jonah prayed unto the LORD his God out of the fish's belly [Jonah 2:1].*

Jonah's prayer was a prayer of thanksgiving, not a prayer for deliverance. Jonah was simply thankful that he had not been drowned. He was delivered in a most spectacular way and was overwhelmed that he had escaped certain death. Even from inside the fish, Jonah's prayer was heard by God. We can pray anywhere and at any time and God will hear us. Your sin is never too great, your predicament never too difficult, for God. Jonah said, "When my soul fainted within me I remembered the *LORD*." Often we act the same way. When life is going well we tend to take God for granted, but when we lose hope, we cry out to Him. This kind of relationship with God can result only in an inconsistent, up-and-down spiritual life. A consistent, daily commitment to God promotes a solid relationship with Him. Look to God during both the good and bad times, and you will have a stronger spiritual life.

> *Again I say unto you, That if two of you shall agree on earth as touching any thing that they shall ask, it shall be done for them of my Father which is in heaven. For where two or three are gather in my name, there am I in the midst of them [Matthew 18:19-20].*

Jesus looked ahead to a new day when He would be present with His followers not in body, but through His Holy Spirit. In the body of believers (the church), the sincere agreement of two people is more powerful than the superficial agreement of thousands, because Christ's Holy Spirit is with them. Two or more believers, *filled with the Holy Ghost*, will pray according to God's will, not their will; and thus their requests will be granted. Can I ask for anything? God does not grant requests that would hurt us or others or that violate His own nature or will. Our requests must be in harmony with the principles of God's Kingdom. The stronger our belief, the more likely our prayers will be in line with God's will, and then God will be happy to grant them.

The Battle

> *And in the morning, rising up a great while before day, we went out, and departed into a solitary place, and there prayed [Mark 2:35].*

Were the disciples impatient that Jesus prayed in solitude while so many ministries waited to be done? How would you have responded if you had been the one to find Jesus in prayer? It's easy to be so caught up with ministry that you neglect times of solitude, individual worship, and prayer. Perhaps you need to redesign your schedule to find time for earnest prayer. It is vitally important to: (1) seek the Lord before your busy schedule takes over your thoughts; (2) withdraw from noise and demands so you can focus on God; (3) take Jesus' attitude of regular communion with the Father; (4) reflect on the priorities Jesus had for his life; (5) determine to pray on a more regular basis, not just in times of crisis. If prayer was important for Jesus, then it must be important for His followers. Pray—even if you have to get up very early in the morning to do it. Start your day with pray.

For many, God had become a symbol of good fortune, a lucky charm, or a magician. Instead of desiring God's pardon and love, they only wanted physical healing or a chance to see spectacular events. Some people still see God as a cosmic magician and prayer as a way to get him to do His tricks. But God is not a magician—He is the Master. Prayer is not a way for us to control Him; it is a way for us to put ourselves under His control.

Christian service has no unemployment. God has work enough for everyone. Jesus encouraged the disciples not just to do the work but also to pray for workers. Part of every missionary's job is to pray for new workers and to help newcomers learn the ropes. Believers are not always to work alone. God wants them to pray, recruit, and equip others to join them as they explore opportunities to serve Jesus. Some people, as soon as they understand the gospel, want to go to convert people immediately. Jesus gave a different approach: begin by mobilizing people to pray. And before praying for unsaved people, pray that other concerned disciples will join you in reaching out to them. God will lead you to an important responsibility, but prayer comes first. God want us to be persisting in prayer until the answer comes. But He does not mean endless repetition or painfully long prayer sessions. Always praying means keeping our requests constantly before God as we live for Him day by day, always believing He will answer. When we thus live by faith, we are not to give up. God may delay answering, but His delays always have good reasons. As we persist in prayer we grow in character, faith, and hope.

From this text, we learn how important it is to God for us to pray and that the world is a tremendous battleground where the forces under Satin's power and those under God's authority are at war. Satan and his forces are motivated by bitter hatred for Christ and His forces. Jesus prayed for his disciples, including those of us who follow Him today. He prayed that God would keep His chosen believers safe from satin's power, making them pure and holy, uniting them through His truth. Jesus prayed for all who would follow Him, including you and me.

Praying Without Ceasing

Our joy, prayers, and thankfulness to God should not fluctuate with our circumstances or feelings. Obeying these three commands—rejoice, keep on praying, and give thanks—often goes against our natural inclinations. When we make a conscious decision to do what God says we will begin to see people in a new perspective. When we do God's will, we will find it easier to be joyful and thankful.

We cannot spend all our time on our knees, but it is possible to have a prayerful attitude at all times. This attitude is built upon acknowledging our dependence on God, realizing His presence within us, and determining to obey Him fully. We then find it natural to pray frequent, spontaneous, short prayers. A prayerful attitude is not a substitute for regular times of prayer but should be an outgrowth of those times.

We should not thank God for everything that happens to us, but in every thing give God thanks. God is not evil. So, we should not thank Him for anything evil.

But when evil strikes, we can still be thankful for God's presence and for the good he will accomplish through the distress.

After 40 days with His disciples, Jesus ascended into heaven. It was important for the disciples to see Jesus taken up into heaven; they knew without a doubt that He was God and that His home was in heaven. Two angels proclaimed to the disciples that one day Jesus would return in the same way He had gone—bodily and visibly. History is not haphazard; it is moving toward a specific point—the return of Jesus to judge and rule over the earth. We should be ready for His sudden return, not by standing around "gazing up into heaven," but by working hard to share the Gospel so that others will be able to share in God's great blessings.

After Christ ascended into heaven, the disciples immediately returned to Jerusalem and had a prayer meeting. Jesus had said they would be baptized with the Holy Spirit in a few days, so they waited and prayed. When you face a difficult task, an important decision, or a baffling dilemma, don't rush into the work or just hope for a good outcome. Instead, make your first step prayer, pray for the Holy Spirit's power and guidance.

At this time, Jesus' brothers were with the disciples. During Jesus' lifetime, they had not believed He was the Messiah, but His resurrection must have convinced them. Jesus' special appearance to James, one of His brothers, may have been an especially significant event in their conversion. This was the first church business meeting. The small group of 11 had already grown to more than 120. The main order of business was to appoint a new disciple, or apostle, as the 11 were now called. While the apostles waited, they were doing what they could—praying, seeking God's guidance, and getting organized. Waiting for God to work does not mean sitting around doing nothing. We must do what we can, while we can, as long as we don't run ahead of God.

We may sometimes be afraid to share our faith in Christ because people might feel uncomfortable or reject us. *For we cannot but speak the things which we have seen and heard [Acts 4:20].* But Peter and John's zeal for the Lord was so strong that they could not keep quiet, even when threatened. If your courage to witness for God has weakened, pray that your boldness may increase. Remember Jesus' promise, "Whosoever therefore shall confess me before men, him will I confess also before my Father which is in heaven."

Notice how the believers prayed. First they praised God; then they told God their specific problem and asked for his help. *And when they heard that, they lifted up their voice to God with one accord, and said, Lord, thou art God, which hast made heaven, and earth, and the sea, and all that in them is [Acts 4:24].* They did not ask God to remove the problem but to help them deal with it. We can follow this model when we pray. We may ask God to remove our problem, and He may choose to do so. But we must recognize that often He will leave a problem in place but give us the strength and courage to deal with it.

> *And when he had considered the thing, he came to the house of Mary the mother of John, whose surname was Mark; where many were gathered together praying. And as Peter knocked at the door of the gate, a damsel came to hearken, name Rhoda. And when she knew Peter's voice, she opened not the gate for gladness, but ran in, and told how Peter stood before the gate [Acts 12:12-14].*

John Mark wrote the Gospel of Mark. His mother's house was large enough to accommodate a meeting of many believers. An upstairs room in this house may have been the location of Jesus' Last Supper with his disciples.

The prayers of the group of believers were answered, even as they prayed. But when the answer arrived at the door, they didn't believe it. We should be people of faith who believe that God answers the prayers of those who seek his will. When you pray, believe you'll get an answer—and when the answer comes, don't be surprised; be thankful!

When you pray continually about a concern, don't be surprised at how God answers. Paul prayed to visit Rome so he could teach the Christians there. When he finally arrived in Rome, it was as a prisoner. Paul prayed for a safe trip, and he did arrive safely—after getting arrested, slapped in the face, shipwrecked, and bitten by a poisonous snake. When you sincerely pray, God will answer—although sometimes in timing and in ways you do not expect.

But when the fullness of the time was come, God sent forth his Son, made of a woman, made *under the law [Galatians 4:4].*

When the fullness of the time was come," God sent Jesus to earth to die for our sins. For centuries the Jews had been wondering when their Messiah would come—but God's timing was perfect. We may sometimes wonder if God will ever respond to our prayers. But we must never doubt him or give up hope. At the right time he will respond. Are you waiting for God's timing? Trust His judgment for your best interests.

> *For this cause we also, since the day we heard it, do not cease to pray for you, and to desire that ye might be filled with the knowledge of his will in all wisdom and spiritual understanding [Colossians 1:9].*

Paul was exposing a heresy in the Colossian church that was a forerunner of Gnosticism. Gnostics valued the accumulation of knowledge, but Paul pointed out that knowledge in itself is empty. To be worth anything, it must lead to a changed life and right living. His prayer for the Colossians has two dimensions—that they might *understand* what God wants, and that they might also have the power to do God's will. Knowledge is not merely to be accumulated; it should give us direction for living. Paul wanted the Colossians to be wise, but he also wanted them to use their knowledge. Knowledge of God is not a secret that only a few can discover; it is open to everyone. God wants us not only to learn more about him, but also to put belief into practice by helping others.

Sometimes we wonder how to pray for missionaries and other leaders we have never met. Paul had never met the Colossians, but he faithfully prayed for them. His prayers teach us how to pray for others, whether we know them or not. We can request that they (1) understand God's will, (2) gain spiritual wisdom, (3) please and honor God, (4) do kind things for others, (5) know God better and better, (6) be filled with God's strength, (7) endure in faith, (8) stay full of Christ's joy, and (9) always be thankful. All believers have these same basic needs. When you don't know how to pray for someone, remember Paul's prayer pattern for the Colossians.

> *I exhort therefore, that, first of all, supplications, prayers, intercessions, and giving of thanks, be made for all men [1 Timothy 2:1].*

Although God is all-powerful and all-knowing, he has chosen to let us help him change the world through our prayers. How this works is a mystery to us because of our limited understanding, but it is a reality. Paul based his instruction about prayer for everyone on his conviction that God's invitation for salvation extends equally to all people. The words "all men" (all people) captures the nature of the Gospel. The world that God loves includes every person. He loves us as individuals whom he knows intimately. Paul urges us to pray for each other and for our leaders in the government. Our earnest prayers will have powerful results.

We should pray for those in authority around the world so that their societies will be conducive to the spread of the Good News. Paul's command to pray for kings is remarkable considering that Nero was emperor at this time and persecution was a growing threat to believers. Nero was a notoriously cruel ruler. Just a short time after Paul wrote this, Nero needed a scapegoat for the great fire that destroyed much of Rome in A.D. 64; he blamed the Roman Christians so as to take the focus off himself. Then persecution erupted throughout the Roman Empire. Not only were Christians denied certain privileges in society, some were even publicly butchered, burned, or fed to animals.

Besides being displeasing to God, it is difficult to pray when we have sinned or when we feel angry and resentful. That is why Jesus told us to interrupt worship, if necessary, to make peace with others. Our goal should be to have a right relationship with God and also with others.

> *I will therefore that men pray every where, lifting up holy hands, without wrath and doubting [1 Timothy 2:8].*
>
> *From whence come wars and fighting among you? come they not hence, even of your lusts that war in your members? Ye lust, and have not: ye kill, and desire to have, and cannot obtain: ye fight and war, yet ye have not, because ye ask not. Ye ask, and receive not, because ye ask amiss, that ye may consume it upon your lusts [James 4:1-3].*

Quarrels ("wars and fighting's") among believers are always harmful. James tells us that these quarrels result from evil desires within us—we want more possessions, more money, higher status, more recognition. When we don't get what we want, we fight in order to have it. Instead of aggressively grabbing what we want, we should ask God to help us get rid of our selfish desires and trust Him to give us what we really need. James mentions the most common problems in pray: not asking, asking for the wrong things, asking for the wrong reason. Do you talk to God at all? When you do, what do you talk about? Do you ask only to satisfy your desires? Do you seek God's approval for what you already plan to do? Your prayers will become powerful when you allow God to change your desires so that they perfectly correspond to His will for you.

> *Is any among you afflicted? Let him pray, Is any merry? Let him sing psalms. Is any sick among you? let him call for the elders of the church; and let them pray over him, anointing him with oil in the name of the Lord: and the prayer of faith shall save the sick, and the Lord shall raise him up; and if he have committed sins, they shall be forgiven him [James 5:13-15].*

James refers to someone who is incapacitated physically. In Scripture, oil was both a medicine and a symbol of the Spirit of God. Oil can represent both the medical and the spiritual spheres of life. Christians should not separate the physical and the spiritual, Jesus Christ is Lord over both the body and the spirit. People in the church are not alone. Members of Christ's body should be able to count on others for support and prayer, especially when they are sick of suffering. The elders should be on call to respond to the illness of any member, and the church should stay alert to pray for the needs of all its members.

"The prayer of faith" does not refer to the faith of the sick person, but to the faith of the people praying. God heals, faith doesn't and all prayers are subject to God's will. But our prayers are part of God's healing process.

"Confess your faults" can be translated "confess your sins." Christ has made it possible for us to go directly to God for forgiveness, but confessing our sins to one another still has an important place in the life of the church. (1) If we have sinned against an individual, we must ask him or her to forgive us. (2) If our sin has affected the church, we must confess it publicly. (3) If we need loving support as we struggle with a sin, we should confess it to those who are able to provide that support. (4) If, after confessing a private sin to God, we still don't feel His forgiveness, we may wish to confess that sin to a fellow believer and hear him or her assure us of God's pardon. In Christ's Kingdom, every believer is a priest to other believers. We must help others come to Christ and tell them of Christ's forgiveness.

The Christian's most powerful resource is communion with God through prayer. The results are often greater than we thought were possible. Some people see prayer as a last resort to be tried when all else fails. This is backwards. Prayer should come first. Since God's power is infinitely greater than our own, it only makes sense to rely on it—especially because He encourages us to do so.

In our fallen world, it is often acceptable to tear people down verbally or get back at them if we feel hurt. Remembering Jesus' teaching to turn the other cheek, encourages His readers to pay back wrongs by praying for the offenders. In God's Kingdom, revenge is unacceptable behavior. So is insulting a person, no matter how indirectly it is done. Rise above getting back at those who hurt you. Instead of reacting angrily to these people, pray for them.

By now someone is asking what is prayer? Why pray? Prayer is asking and receiving; it is talking with God. It is making your request known to Him in faith. Our Lord instructs the believer to ask, seek, and knock; because these three words cover the whole spectrum of prayer.

(1) Prayer is asking and receiving. When you know the will of God regarding a need, whether it is material or spiritual,

you can ask and receive. This is prayer according to the revealed will of God.

(2) Prayer is seeking and finding. When you do not know the will of God regarding a need, whether it is material of spiritual, then you are to seek His will in prayer concerning this need until you find it. This is prayer for knowledge of the unrevealed will of God in a specific need.

(3) Prayer is knocking and opening. When you know the will of God, and yet you find a closed door, you are to knock, and keep on knocking until God opens the door. This is tenacious prayer—prayer for mountain—moving faith. Knocking prayer perseveres until the impossible becomes the possible. This is miracle-working prayer. Remember all things are possible when you ask, seek, and knock.

Why pray? (1) Because Jesus said, "Men always ought to pray." Prayer is imperative. You are commanded to pray; (2) prayer is the only way to get things from God. *"You do not have because you do not ask"*; (3) there is joy in prayer; (4) prayer saves in times of trouble; (5) prayer unlocks the treasure chest of God's wisdom; (6) prayer is a channel of power; (7) it is a sin not to pray; (8) sinners can be saved when they pray in faith; (9) Jesus, while here in the flesh, prayed often to the Father. If Jesus, the Son of God, needed to pray, then we should *"pray without ceasing."*

Praying to our Heavenly Father, in the Name of Jesus Christ, using God's Holy Word (*scripture*) in prayer is the most powerful thing we can do for ourselves and others.

The heart of prayer is the Will of our Heavenly Father. Part of that Will is simply coming to Him. He desires us, as His dear children to know Him. He desires your love, your attention, your fellowship (more than just being related to Him through Jesus). He also desires a time of communion, an intimate time of personal exchange and involvement, and finally a release of His Will and manifest Presence in the earth through prayer.

As you pray for your needs and the needs of others, you are actually becoming a prayer warrior, an intercessor, just as Jesus was and is today for each of us. Jesus is constantly interceding for us to our Heavenly Father. It is written that Jesus was sent to destroy the works of the devil. We are to do the same. We have the power and authority through Jesus Christ. All we have to do is live in the promise of the Word of God and to use His precious Name.

The most powerful weapons we have are the Name of Jesus Christ and God's Holy Word against, Satan and his foul wicked demons. No power of darkness can stand against the Word of God in the Name of Jesus Christ, and through the Blood of Jesus Christ.

We are instructed to pray in all places at all times. It is a great joy to be able to talk with God, any time, any place, under any condition, and to know that He will hear and answer. When prayers are not answered, you should examine yourself in the light of God's Word. If you find anything not pleasing to God, confess it, believing God for forgiveness that your prayers may be answered.

(1) An unharmonious relationship between husband and wife will hinder prayer.
(2) Selfishness will hinder prayer.
(3) An unforgiving spirit will hinder prayer. Many Christians go without answers to prayer because they have wronged others, or have been wronged and have failed to humble themselves and seek reconciliation.
(4) Unbelief will hinder prayer.
(5) Known sin in the heart will hinder prayer. When you pray, go to God in all humility. Ask Him to reveal anything in your life that is not pleasing to Him. Then judge it; confess it, calling it by name and forsake it. Pray in all simplicity and earnestness, believing, and God will hear and answer.

I knew that God had called me to preach His word, but I had to learn that God answers prayer in His own way and in His own time. If you want to have your prayers answered, you must be open to what God can do in impossible situations. And you must wait for God to work in His way and in His time.

I was reading about Mary the mother of Jesus. Mary was young, poor; female-all characteristics that, to the poor of her day, would make her seem unusable by God for any major task. But God chose Mary for one of the most important acts of obedience He has ever demanded of anyone. You may feel that your ability, experience, or education make you an unlikely candidate for God's service. Do not limit God's choices. He can use you if you trust Him.

God's favor does not automatically bring instant success or fame. His blessing on Mary, the honor of being the mother of the Messiah, would lead to much pain: Her peers would ridicule her; her fiancé would come close to leaving her; her son would be rejected and murdered. But through her son came the world's only hope and this is why Mary has been praised by countless generations as "blessed among women." Her submission led to our salvation. If sorrow weighs you down and dims your hope, think of Mary and wait patiently for God to finish working out His plan.

The birth of Jesus to a virgin is a miracle that many people find hard to believe. These three facts can aid our faith: (1) Luke was a medical doctor, and he knew perfectly well how babies are made. It would have been just as hard for him to believe in a virgin birth as it is for us, yet he reports as fact. (2) Luke was a pain taking researcher who based his Gospel on eyewitness accounts. Tradition holds that he talked with Mary about the events. This is her story, not a fictional invention. (3) Christians and Jews, who worship God as the Creator of the universe, should believe He has the power to create a child in a virgin's womb. And Mary, with her story about being made pregnant by the Holy Spirit, risked being considered crazy as well. Still she said, despite the possible risks, "Be it unto me according to thy word." When Mary said that, she didn't know about the tremendous opportunity she would have. She only knew God was asking her to serve Him, and she willingly obeyed. Don't wait to see the bottom line before offering your life to God. Offer yourself willingly, even when the outcome seems disastrous.

God promises that His harvest will be magnificent and prolific-the best fruit ever grown. Your witness may be weak and your efforts may seem to influence so few, but the Word of God is a powerful growth agent. Keep your eyes on the great harvest to come and do not let bad soil or weeds discourage you from faithful service and witness.

Sometimes our trouble or pain is so great that all we can do is cry out to God, "Preserve my soul" or "Protect me." We feel so poor and needy. Many times when there is no relief in sight, all we can do is acknowledge the greatness of God and wait for better days ahead. The conviction that God answers prayer will sustain us in such difficult times.

God does not listen to our prayers if we intend to go back to our sin as soon as we get off our knees. If we want to forsake our sin and follow Him, however, He willingly listens-no matter how bad our sin has been. What closes His ears is not the depth of our sin, but our secret intention to do it again. God hears our intentions as clearly as He hears our words.

Most of us pray only when all else fails. We need to have a regular, earnest and persistent prayer life. Our prayer should be more than a few words each day. It should be embodied within us, changing us. We must not be content with where we are spiritually. The Lord God wants us to continue to grow in our understanding of and love for Him. That is why we must press on by daily surrender in prayers. Worshipful prayer goes beyond a mere daily routine. The Lord would like to guide us during every step of our day; all we have to do is listen to Him. Watching and praying enables us to hear His voice clearly. Then we get to know the heart of God, to become more intimate with Him.

You do not have, because you do not ask God [James 4:2]

We go through three stages as we develop our prayer life. First, we are disciplined in our prayers, then our prayer becomes heartfelt and, finally, our whole beings are consumed by our relationship in prayer with the Lord.

Prayer requires discipline. We discipline our bodies to become athletes. In the same way, it is important to focus on growing closer to God through prayer. It requires practice and effort-conditioning. The disciplined prayer life is when we set up times for just praying.

It may be liturgical prayer or conversational prayer, but we begin to develop a discipline with praying.

It always has been easier for me to improve the condition of my body than to bring my soul into subjection. It is much easier for me to *do* things for the Lord than to *submit* to Him—to recognize Him as all-important and sovereign. It is a discipline to align ourselves to be with God and only God, to be intimate with Him, to know Him and for Him to know us. This is the intimacy of being a Christian.

Focusing on what I do best has enabled me to become more fervent in my prayer. Christians are commanded to fight slothfulness and to be faithful and focused. It is important to do one thing at a time and to do it well. Dr. James Gills stated, "In my ophthalmology practice, I have worked hard to narrow my specialty and remain focused on procedures I do best and with fewer complications. The days that I have the most work on my calendar are the days I need to pray more. Days that I am disciplined, I make a stronger effort to pray and stay in the Word is the days that flow in my life."

> *I will praise the Lord, who counsels me; even at night my heart instructs me. I have set the Lord always before me. Because he is at my right hand, I will not be shaken [Psalm 16:7-8].*

Many people in the Bible were disciplined and set aside three times to pray during the day. Even the old Jewish prayers were not enough, and in the New Testament the disciples asked, "Lord teach us to pray." They realized the disciplined prayer life of the Old Testament wasn't adequate.

So the second stage is taking prayer beyond the times we set aside and making prayer an integral part of our daily life. Just as the motor skills we use to play or do our jobs become ingrained responses, so it should be with our prayer life. We have an increasing awareness of God and our need for His direction daily in our life. Our active faith in God is reflected in a soul engaged in constant meditation with our Redeemer. Our hearts are so directed toward God that we are being directed by Him and not by the world.

Our prayer now becomes heartfelt. Everything that is within us cries out for the Lord. The joy that comes from our relationship with the Lord overcomes us. When we know God as both immanent (near us) and transcendent (all powerful), our prayer life is constant. It is just like talking to another person on Earth.

A variety of thoughts go between us and the Lord, and the Lord is one with us. We don't have to pray in showy, ostentatious, demanding or pushy ways. We simply think and talk to the Lord.

We are not looking for dramatic events to hive us more faith in God. We're merely in communion with our closest friend. That relationship gives us a peace as we live our life on Earth and a sense of joy and purpose in our life.

When every bit of energy we have is turned toward the Lord, we've reached the third stage—whole self prayer. Everything we have thank God in prayer. The prayerful spirit becomes so pervasive in our life that our soul is intertwined with prayer. Prayer becomes so integrated in our life that it is like dew. Our life is scented by it. Our prayers extend not just in our head but throughout our body. I believe prayers are examples of the thoughts that extend through our whole being: "Lord, baptize me with love," "Teach me gentleness, Father." "Teach me patience, Father." "Lord Jesus, help me feel loved and help me love."

> *I waited patiently for the Lord; he turned to me and heard my cry [Psalm 40:1].*

We know God answers prayers, but there are times we want Him to follow our own timetable and not His. When we are impatient, we begin to lose faith that He will answer us or will not give us what we want, so we try to take matters into our own hands. We battle God for control of our lives. Instead, we need to have faith that He will provide for us because He loves us, but for His glory and not our own.

Failure to wait on God greatly hinders our relationship with Him. And impatience, in direct opposition to God's commands, may even lead to more sin. Psalm 27:14 gives us confidence when we get impatient: "*Wait for the Lord; be strong and take heart and wait for the*

Lord." Having confidence and faith that God will provide can get us through many situations in which we want to turn from God and turn to our own solutions.

Prayer is the way to grow closer to our Creator and to align ourselves with His will. Yet no matter how much we desire that relationship and want to show our love for Him, we are never free from obstacles. We must battle our own egos, the agendas of our families and peers, and what the world tells us about success to stay in a relationship of prayer with our Lord.

When we are aligned with God, our priorities are in line with His will, and we feel loved and protected. When we get away from God, we start to feel sorry for ourselves when times get rough. We begin to believe we are not getting the love or recognition we deserve.

When we align ourselves with the pull of worldly influences, we no longer are controlled by the Lord. We find ourselves being selfish, covetous, proud and uncaring. Then we become irrational and start making bad decisions based on worry or fear. We worry that we are not getting ahead quickly enough in our careers or in the accumulation of worldly possessions. We are afraid of what others might say or think of us. We buy into the world's view of success and join the *"rat race."* We base our decisions and actions on pleasing others. *James 3:16 says, "For where you have envy and selfish ambition, there you find disorder and every evil practice."*

How does all this happen? Can it happen if we are in communion with God? No matter how strong our spirit is, as long as we are housed in earthly temples, we will always struggle to overcome the weaknesses of the flesh, we will struggle against our egos, the demands of our jobs and families, and the temptations Satan puts in our path.

The humility that is so necessary for our salvation is so often gone. The humility that is so necessary for our being filled with the Holy Spirit is so often not present. There is no way we can be filled with the Holy Spirit and the Word and pray passionately and deeply until we have emptied ourselves of pride and the things that go along with it, such as the desire for wealth and power.

To keep us from succumbing to the subtle temptations that pull us away from God, we must deny ourselves, take up our cross and follow the Lord with all our heart. That may sound easier said than done. But God has given us an example of submitting to His will in the life and death of his Son, Jesus. With every fiber of His being crying for life, Jesus submitted to His father's will and died so that we might live.

Prayer is a key to staying faithful and following His example. Watchful prayer helps us be victorious over those temptations, because during that time with our Lord we receive the guidance and direction that keep us focused on God's will. Then we base our decisions on His will, not our own. And our mind, body and behavior will be inclined to Him in everything we do.

The battle against worldly influences that keep us from a life of prayer is never over. Let us look at some of the pitfalls to prayer and how we can indentify them and fight back.

> *Without faith, it is impossible to please God, because anyone who comes to him must believe that he exists and that he rewards those who earnestly seek him [Hebrews 11:6].*

Faith avoids the burnout and anxieties that occur as we live and struggle in this competitive world. Faith is our response to Christ. We must live a life of faith knowing that the Lord provides and takes care of us. His grace is sufficient for everything.

Yet there are still times when we doubt God and His Word. We can be limited in our relationship of prayer when we do not see the expanse of God. We can fail to look at Him with all our heart and, in our whole being, have faith in Him. Even the disciples, who lived and walked with Jesus and saw Him perform many miracles, doubted Him.

We can be the same way, walking along in faith until we see the storm around us. Then we get scared and want to take charge. We begin to sink in our troubles because we have taken our eyes off our Lord. God knows it requires faith to believe in Him and put total trust and total control of our life in His hands. Faith comes by hearing the Word of God. It is our response to hearing that Word and using it in our lives. He also reassures us of the blessings we receive when we do hand Him the reins. Jesus tells the disciples in Mark 20:29, *"Because you have seen me, you have believed; blessed are those who have not seen and yet have believed."*

Our faith needs to be strong that it doesn't allow the cares of the world to interfere with our lifestyle of prayer. As our faith grows, so grows our ability to let God be in charge, to remember that He is in control and to surrender ourselves to Him. We pray with confidence that He hears our prayers and will provide for us.

Yet when we pray with faith, we must be sure we are not giving God directions. Faith can give way to pride, and we begin to tell God what to do, rather than seeking His will. There are two parts of a person-the controlling side and the caring or nurturing side. Prayer to our Redeemer must bring both parts together so we pray with an attitude of faith, not arrogance. If faith does not represent our relationship with God, then our relationship is superficial.

> *And what does the Lord require of you? To act justly and to love mercy and to walk humbly with your God [Micah 6:8].*

Pride is one of the biggest roadblocks to prayer. When we begin to think we can do things ourselves, when we want to be independent and put ourselves first, we do not live a lifestyle of a lifestyle of surrender to our Lord. And when we think we can handle things ourselves, we begin to stop relying on God and seeking Him in prayer.

Lucifer gives us the most powerful example of what can happen when pride overtakes us.

> *You were anointed as a guardian cherub, for so I ordained you. You were on the holy mount of God; you walked among the fiery stones. You were blameless in your ways from the day you were created till wickedness was found in you [Ezekiel 28:14-15].*

Lucifer walked closest to the throne of the Almighty until he became prideful and wanted to take God's place. This pride led to Lucifer's rebellion against God and to his ruin. Closely associated with pride is the independence Lucifer showed when he said, "I will do this," and" I will do that." An independent spirit will not long be tolerated in the presence of God. Wanting to rely on our own skills and abilities to succeed adds up to sin. We leave our attitudes of independence and pride behind when we realize we can not live without prayer.

As teenagers, we all wanted to be grown up and out on our own in the world—independent from our families and God, making our own way and making our own decisions. We battle the same attitude in our relationship with our Father. But this is the opposite of what Jesus tells us. Being independent separates us from the Lord and his power. Jesus says:

> *I am the vine; you are the branches. If a man remains in me and I in him, he will bear much fruit; apart from me you can do nothing. If anyone does not remain in me, he is like a branch that is thrown away and withers; such branches are picked up, thrown into the fire and burned. If you remain in me and my words remain in you, ask whatever you wish, and it will be given* you [John 15:5-7].

Our dependence on Him increases as we commune with our Lord more in prayer. Then His will becomes our will. His desires become our desires. His standard of success becomes ours. The only coping mechanism I have when I am overwhelmed by the daily battle is to relax in the Lord instead of trying to fix everything myself. **Proverbs tells us that pride comes before a fall.** An important part of being a good Christian is being humble first. It is essential to be humble, dependent and totally filled with the Holy Spirit to shear the healing power that comes from God.

Frequently when we are disappointed with ourselves, we project that disappointment to others. That disappointment leads to anger and the anger to depression. We lash out against what we now perceive as the problem—the other person. We project our unfaithfulness, our sins, and all our problems on others rather than trying to clear them up and restore our inner peace.

We can do the same thing to God. We can blame Him for our disappointments, for feeling betrayed, for being unfaithful, when the blame really falls on our shoulders. Through prayer we can keep our desires aligned with God's will for our life. When we are in communion with Him, our heart is inclined to His, and we trust that He will take care of us. We no longer need to worry about providing for ourselves. He will provide.

Once we put our faith in Him, we realize how dependent we are on Him. Our own efforts pale in comparison with the power of the Almighty, and we are humble in His presence. We are happy serving the Lord, and He will bless us. Jesus tells us in Luke 14:11, *"For everyone who exalts himself will be humbled, and he who humbles himself will be exalted."*

I waited patiently for the Lord; he turned to me and heard my cry [Psalm 40:1].

We know God answers prayers, but there are times we want Him to follow our own timetable and not His. When we are impatient, we begin to lose faith that He will answer us or will not give us what we want, so we try to take matters into our own hands. We battle God for control of our lives. Instead, we need to have faith that He will provide for us because He loves us, but for His glory and not our own.

Give thanks in all circumstances, for this is God's will for you in Christ Jesus [1 Thessalonians 5:18]

Prayer should change us by our thanksgiving, by our rejoicing in our Creator. We should want to give thanks for all God has provided us and all the difficult times we face. I thank the Lord each day for my life, for my health and for my strength. I thank Him for my family, my friends and my ministry. I thank Him for the bad days as well as the good days.

The Lord Is Merciful

And he said, I beseech thee, shew me thy glory [Exodus 33:18].

Moses wanted to see God's glory. Because we are finite and morally imperfect, we cannot exist and see God as He is. To see God's "back parts" means we can only see where God has passed by. We can only know Him by what He does and How he acts. We cannot comprehend God as He really is apart from Jesus Christ. What is God's glory? It is His character, His nature, His way of relating to His creatures. God did not give Moses a vision of His power and majesty, but rather of His love. God's glory is revealed in His mercy, grace, longsuffering, goodness, truth, forgiveness and justice. God's love and mercy are truly wonderful, and we benefit from them.

Moses' face actually glowed after he spent time with God. The people could clearly see God's presence in Him. How often do you spend time alone with God? Time spent in prayer, reading the Bible, and meditating should have such an effect on your life that people will know you have been with God.

God puts no limit on the number of times we can come to Him to obtain mercy, but we must come in order to obtain it, recognizing our need and asking Him for help. *"Thou art a gracious and merciful God!"* If there is a recurring problem or difficulty in your life, continue to ask God for help, and be willing and ready to make changes in your attitude and behavior that will correct that difficulty.

God wants to carry our burdens, but often we continue to bear them ourselves even when we say we are trust Him. Trust the same strength that sustains you to also carry your burdens. HOW MUCH HARM CAN PEOPLE DO TO US? They can inflict pain, suffering, and death. But no person can rob us of our souls or our future beyond this life. How much harm can we do to ourselves? The worst thing we can do is to reject God and lose our eternal future. Jesus said, *"Fear not them which kill the body, but are not able to kill the soul."* **Instead, we should fear God, who controls this life and the next.**

Even in our deepest sorrow, God cares! Jesus reminded us further of how much God understands us-he knows even the number of hairs on our heads. Often we waver between faith and fear. When you feel so discouraged that you are sure no one understands, remember that God knows every problem and sees every tear.

At times, we may be surrounded by people who gossip about us or criticize us. Verbal cruelty can damage us as badly as physical abuse. Rather than throwing back more unacceptable talk, we, can quietly talk with God about the problem. During sleepless, uncomfortable nights, just think about God. Instead of counting sheep, just meditate on Jesus. Review all the ways God had already helped you, and the next day get up with songs of praise. In quiet moments or wakeful nights, make it a point to count examples of God's faithfulness to you. Doing so is far more likely to give you rest than any other items you might count!

> *Justice and judgment are the habitation of thy throne: mercy and truth shall go before thy face. Blessed is the people that know the joyful sound: they shall walk, O LORD, in the light of thy countenance [Psalm 89:14-15].*

Righteousness and justice, mercy and truth surround God on His throne; they are central characteristics of the way God rules. They summarize His character. As God's ambassadors, we should exhibit the same traits when we deal with people. Make sure your actions flow out of justice, righteousness, mercy, and truth because any unfair, unloving, or dishonest action cannot come for God.

You may be angry at being attacked by evil people who slandered you and lied. Yet you have got to love your enemies and pray for them. While we must hate evil and work to overcome it, we must love everyone, including those who do evil, because God loves them. We are called to hate the sin, but love the person. Only through God's strength will we be able to follow this example.

We must learn to be peacemakers. A peacemaker is not always popular. Some people prefer to fight for what they believe in. The glory of battle is in the hope of winning, but someone must be a loser. The glory of peacemaking is that it may actually produce two winners. Peacemaking is God's way, so we should carefully and prayerfully attempt to be peacemakers.

Making iniquities-holding a grudge-is like building a wall between you and another person, and it is nearly impossible to talk openly while the wall is there. God never holds a grudge; when he forgives, he forgives completely, tearing down any wall between Him and us. Therefore, we can talk to Him about anything. When you pray, realize that God is holding nothing against you. His lines of communication are completely open.

Two important character qualities are mercy and truthfulness. Both involve actions as well as attitudes. A merciful person not only feels love, he also acts responsibly and faithfully. A truthful person not only believes the truth, he also works for justice for others. Thoughts and words are not enough-our lives reveal whether we are truly merciful and truthful. Do your actions measure up to your attitudes?

Paul offers a strategy to help us live for God day by day: (1) Imitate-Christ's merciful, forgiving attitude; (2) let love ("charity") guide your life; (3) let the peace of God rule in your heart; (4) always be thankful; (5) keep God's Word in you at all times; (6) live as Jesus Christ's representative.

The key to forgiving others is remembering how much God has forgiving you. Is it difficult for you to forgive someone who has wronged you a little when God has forgiven you so much? Realizing

God's infinite love and forgiveness can help you love and forgive others. Let God worry about the wrongs you have suffered. Do not quench your life in bitter feuding; live renewed in love and joy. God want people to turn to Him while there is still time. Time is running out and destruction will soon be upon us. Because we do not know when our lives will end, we should turn to the Lord now, while we can. Do not let anything hold you back from turning to God. Television and movies are filled with images of people who seem to have no fear. Many today have modeled their lives after these images-they want to be tough at any cost. But God is not impressed with tough actions. He says that even the toughest of man will run in fear when God's judgment comes. Can you think of people who consider themselves tough enough to make it with or without God? Don't be swayed by their self-assured rhetoric. Recognize that God fears no one, and one day all people will fear Him.

Even in anger, God is merciful: He always warned His people through prophets before punishing them. Warnings about sin and judgment apply to people today just as they did to Israel. If we have been warned about our sin, we have no excuse when punishment comes. God had warned his people through His prophets, so they could not rationalize or complain when He punished them for refusing to repent. Do not take lightly warnings in God's Word about judgment. His warnings are a way of showing mercy to you. Israel had forgotten how to do what was right. The more they sinned, the harder it was to remember what God wanted. The same is true for us. The longer we fail to deal with sin, the greater its hold on us. Finally, we forget what it means to do right. Are you on the verge of forgetting?

No matter how God warned the people-through famines, earthquakes, drought, blight, storms, or war-they still ignored Him. Because they did not get the message, they will have to meet Him face-to-face in judgment. No longer would they ignore God; they will have to face the One they had rejected, the One they had refused to obey when He commanded them to care for the poor. One day each of us will meet God face-to-face to account for what we have done or refused to do. Have you listened to His Word? Are you prepared to meet Him?

There is one sure remedy for a world that is sick and dying in sin-seek God and live. Sin seeks to destroy, but hope is found in seeking God. In times of difficulty, seek God. In personal discomfort and struggle, seek God. When others are struggling, encourage them to seek God too. We must not assume that going to church and being good is enough, God expects our belief in Him to penetrate all areas of our lives and extend to all people and circumstances.

Sometimes people wish that judgment and destruction would come upon sinful people whose wickedness seems to demand immediate punishment. But God is more merciful than we can imagine. He feels compassion for the sinners we want judged, and he devises plans to bring them to Himself. What is your attitude toward those who are especially wicked? Do you want them destroyed? Or do you wish they could experience God's mercy and forgiveness?

God spared the sailors when they pleaded for mercy. God saved Jonah when he prated from the belly of the fish. God saved the people of Nineveh when they responded to Jonah's preaching. God answers the prayers of those who call upon Him. God will always work His will, and He desires that all come to Him, trust in Him, and be saved. We can be saved if we heed God's warning to us through His Word. If we respond in obedience, He will be gracious, and we will receive His mercy, not His judgment.

God loves to be merciful! He does not forgive grudgingly, but is glad when we repent and offers forgiveness to all who come back to Him. Today you can confess your sins and receive His loving forgiveness. Do not be too proud to accept God's free offer.

People have tried all kinds of ways to please God, but God has made his wishes clear. He wants His people to be fair, just, and merciful, and to walk humbly with Him. In your efforts to please God, examine these areas on a regular basis. Are you fair in your dealings with people? Do you show mercy to those who wrong you? Are you learning humility?

To those who refuse to believe, God's punishment is like an angry fire. To those who love Him, His mercy is security and peace, supplying all our needs without diminishing His supply. But to His enemies He is a flood that will sweep them away. The relationship we have is up to us. Which kind of relationship will you choose?

So many people feel guilty and condemned, may I offer you reassurance. When you feel this way, do not give up hope-the best defense attorney in the universe is pleading your case. Jesus Christ, your advocate, is the Judge's Son. He has already suffered your penalty in your place. You can not be tried again for a case that is no longer on the docket. United with Jesus, you are as safe as He is. Do not be afraid to ask Him to plead your case-He has already won it.

Jesus Christ is the "propitiation" or atoning sacrifice for our sins. He is our defense attorney. He can stand before God as our mediator because His death satisfied the wrath of God against sin and paid the death penalty for our sin. Christ both satisfies God's requirement and removes our sin. In Him we are forgiven and cleansed.

We sometimes have a difficult time forgiving someone who wrongs us. Imagine how hard it would be to forgive all people, no matter what they had done! This is what God has done in Jesus. No one, no matter what sin has been committed, is beyond forgiveness. All we have to do is turn from sin, receive Christ's forgiveness, and commit our heart to Him.

How can you be sure you belong to Christ? A Christian should do what Christ tells him or her to do and live as Christ wants you to live. And what does Christ tell us to do? "Believe on the name of His Son Jesus Christ, and love one another." True Christian faith results in loving behavior; **that is why John says our behavior can assure us that we are Christ's.**

> *But whoso keepeth His Word, in him verily is the love of God perfected: hereby know we that we are in Him. He that saith he abideth in Him ought himself also so to walk, even as he walked [1 John 2:5-6].*

Christ lives (abides, dwells) in us, and we also live in Christ. This means we place our total trust in Him and live as He wants us to live. We are "born of God" when the Holy Spirit lives in us and gives us Jesus' new life. Being born again is more than a fresh start; it is a rebirth, receiving a new family name based on Christ's death for us. God forgives us and totally accepts us. The Holy Spirit gives us a new mind and heart, lives in us, and begins helping us be like Christ. Our perspective changes, too. We have a mind that is renewed day by day by the Holy Spirit. So we must begin to think and act differently.

When we become Christians, we receive the Holy Spirit. God's presence in our life is a proof that we really belong to Him. He also gives us the power to love. Rely on that power as you reach out to others. As you do so, you will gain confidence.

The Day of Judgment is that final day when we will appear before Christ and be held accountable for our actions. With God living in us through Christ, we have no reason to fear this day, because we have been saved from punishment. Instead, we can look forward to the Day of Judgment, because it will mean the end of sin and the beginning of a face-to-face relationship with Jesus Christ.

If we are ever afraid of the future, eternity, or God's Judgment, we can remain ourselves of God's love. We know He loves us perfectly. We can resolve our fears first by focusing on His immeasurable love for us, and then by allowing Him to love others through us. His love will quiet your fears and give you confidence.

It is easy to say we love God when it does not cost us anything more than weekly attendance of religious services. But the real test of our love for God is how we treat the people right in front of us-our family members and fellow believers. We cannot truly love God while neglecting to love those who are created in his image.

When we become Christians, we become part of God's family, with fellow believers as our brothers and sisters. It is God who determines who the other family members are, not us. We are simply called to accept and love them. How well do you treat your fellow family members? Jesus never promised that obeying Him would be easy. Hard work, however, can be rewarding if we value its results. "His commands are not burdensome." The hard work and self discipline of serving Christ is no burden to those who love Him. And if our load starts to feel heavy, we can always trust Christ to help us bear it.

Whoever believes in God's Son has eternal life. He is all you need. You do not need to wait for eternal life, because it begins the moment you believe. You do not need to work for it, because it is already yours. You do not need to worry about it, because you have been given eternal life by God Himself, and it is guaranteed. Some people hope they will receive eternal life. We can know we have it. Our certainty is based on God's promise that He has given us eternal life through His Son. This is true whether you feel close to God or distant from Him. Eternal life is not based on feelings, but on facts. You can know you have eternal life if you believe God's truth. If you are not sure that you are a Christian, ask yourself: "Have I honestly committed my life to Him as my Savior and Lord?" If so, you know by faith that you are indeed a child of God.

God is the God of all comfort. Let us carefully look at exactly what that means. Very often, the picture we get of comfort is people feeling sorry for the person who is experiencing trouble. That is not what God does. He is not sitting in heaven feeling sorry for us.

The Scripture tells us: *Blessed be God, even the Father of our Lord Jesus Christ, the Father of mercies, and the God of all comfort; Who comforteth us in all our tribulation, that we may be able to comfort them which are in any trouble, by the comfort wherewith we ourselves are comforted of God 2 Corinthians 1:3, 4.*

To be a comforter means to be one who draws near to those who are afflicted. Notice He's the God of all comfort, and He comforts us in "all our tribulation." God is willing to be your Comforter in life no matter what you go through. He will provide comfort no matter how difficult things seem. He draws near to all those who are facing difficult times in life, and He gives then grace to help in their times of need.

God comforts us so that we can bring that same comfort to others who may be facing similar situations. If you are facing a situation that seems overwhelming, do not give up. God is the God of all comfort. He will provide comfort for you in that situation. Not only that, when it is all said and done, you can impart into others that very comfort which you received.

Although God and Satan are at war, we do not need to wait until the end to see who will win. God has *already* defeated Satan, and when Christ returns, Satan and all he stands for will be eliminated forever. Satan is here now, however, and he is trying to win us over to his evil cause. With the Holy Spirit's power, we can resist Satan and he will flee from us.

How do we resist Satan? *Draw nigh to God, and He will draw nigh to you. Cleanse your hands, ye sinners, and purify your hearts, ye double minded* [James 4:8].

How can we draw close ("nigh") to God? 0(1) "Submit...to God." Realize that you need His forgiveness, and be willing to follow Him. (2) "Resist the devil." Don't allow him to entice and tempt you. (3) "Cleanse your hands...and purify your hearts" (that is, lead a pure life. Be cleansed from sin, replacing it with God's purity. (4) Let there be tears, sorrow, and sincere grief for your sins. Do not be afraid to express deep heartfelt sorrow for them. (5) Humble yourself before God, and He will lift you up.

Humbling ourselves means recognizing that our worth comes from God alone. It is leaning on His power and His guidance, not our own independent effort. Although we do not deserve His favor, He reaches out to us in love and gives us worth and dignity despite our human shortcomings.

When we turn our life over to Christ, when we are born again in faith, our old life dies, and our new life is totally with Christ. Our secret is our love for Him, which changes us. Love and faith combine to make us one with Him.

All we need we are given from God. God gives us freedom from our sins through His grace, and peace from guilt and the troubles of this world. He will supply us all the power in the world as we need it. That gives us strength to live and believe confidently in Him.

> *Therefore, since we have been justified through faith, we have peace with God through our Lord Jesus Christ [Romans 5:1].*

We are brought into Christ, and He becomes our mediator, our lawyer, our counselor. Therefore, we have the peace of reconciliation, and we can enjoy peace with God through our Lord Jesus Christ, the Messiah. Christ is the Anointed One in whom we breathe and live. In our spiritual life we need nothing else. And when we place Christ as our highest priority in our spiritual life, everything else will be taken care of. This brings a change in our life. We no longer live according to what we want to do, but we seek His will because we put Him at the center of our life. We want to do His will in our life.

Our responsibility is to stand our ground as a soldier in Christ, wearing our spiritual armor, as Paul described in Ephesians 6:13-17:

Wherefore take unto you the whole armor of God that ye may be able to withstand in the evil day, and having done all, to stand.

I can remember a time in my life when I felt that I just couldn't stand any longer. I felt as if I had stood for so long that my armor was falling off. When the attacks first started, my sword was sharp, my shield was strong, and all the rest of my armor was intact. I responded to the challenges as a good soldier in Christ. I told the devil, "By Jesus' stripes, I'M healed. My God meets my needs!"

However, after doing this for a long time I got to the point where it seemed as if nothing was working. I felt as if my breastplate was falling off. My shield of faith was so heavy that I couldn't hold it up any longer. I couldn't even see the enemy because my helmet had slipped down over my eyes! I asked God, "what do I do now?' As I said earlier church doors were being close in my face. God said, "Stand." Then I heard Him say this, "Daughter, it's time to rejoice." I though Lord how can I rejoice? My feeling was being hurt just about every Sunday, I was the subject of many churches, I would go to bed many night crying because so many people did not understand what God was doing in life.

But God said to me its time to rejoice, I said what do I have to rejoice about? God do you see me? Do you have any idea what I'm going through? God I can't hold my shield of faith up any longer. Lord there is no more space for another dart. My shield is full of darts. I've even got darts in my helmet!" But Lord you said that I can rejoice.

They that sow in tears shall reap in joy [Psalm 126:5].

God's capacity for restoring life is beyond our understanding. Forests burn down and are able to grow back. Broken bones heal. Even grief is not a permanent condition. Our tears can be seeds that will grow into a harvest of joy because God is able to bring good out of tragedy. When burdened by sorrow, know that your times of grief will end and that you will again find joy. We must be patient as we wait. God's great harvest of joy is coming.

Ultimate joy comes from Christ dwelling within us. The Lord "is at hand," and at His Second Coming we will fully realize this ultimate joy. He who dwells within us will fulfill His final purposes for us.

Jesus had said to His disciple Thomas, who came to believe after touching the resurrected Christ: "Because thou hast seen me, thou believed: blessed are they that have not seen, and yet have believed. Jesus Christ whom we have not seen, ye love. Faith brings both salvation and the promise of a day when pain will end and perfect justice will begin. Faith will be rewarded and evil will be punished. But what should we do until then? The Bible's answer is simple but not easy: Because we know the future, we must faithfully serve God here and now. If today that means resoling a conflict, mending a hurt, or just waiting for guidance-do it all with the joy of God, who will return with His reward!

Have you ever felt like this? Lord my faith is getting weak I need you. If so, it is time to rejoice! It may seem as if you have lost everything. It may look as if you will never get over all the attacks that have been launched against you. I want you to notice this one thing: You are still standing, and for this reason, it is time to rejoice.

Although Satan may have hit you with his best shot, you are still standing, and you must not give up. Keep trusting in God. Keep declaring the Word of God over your situation. You may feel as if you want to put up your hands and say I quit, but continue to stand. It is time to rejoice! You have the devil right where you want him, so straighten up your armor and tell the devil that you will not quit.

In my situation, I finally straightened up my armor and then God said I called you to preach my Words. Let God Be the Judge, I will open doors for you, "Now rejoice." So, I started rejoicing. Just as the apostle Paul said, I was able to stand against the wiles of the devil.

Perhaps you feel as though your armor is falling off. Maybe you don't even know where your armor is. This is not the time to start stripping off what little armor you have left. This is the time to get it back on, tighten it up, and stand. If you will, then you are about to win!

I must say again, our joy, prayers, and thankfulness to God should not fluctuate with our circumstances or feelings. Obeying these three commands- rejoice, keep on praying, and give thanks- often goes against our natural inclinations. When we make a conscious decision to do what God says, however, we will begin to see people in a new perspective. When we do God's will, we will find it easier to be joyful and thankful.

When God call you to do something, do it, Nothing can stop you if you will continue to trust God. No matter how hard the devil tries to keep it from happening, your faith will cause you to overcome everything he throws your way.

Right now is the time to rise up and do what God called you to do. God gave it to you, and it is worth fighting for. Satan does not have the power to steal what God has given you. He cannot take it from you if you won't allow him. When he comes, remind him that you have authority over him. Remind him that there is nothing he can do to stop you from fulfilling what God have called you to do. Remind him that the Lord is a light unto you, and your destiny is in God's hands.

Once again, never give up on what God called you to do. No matter how long it takes, no matter what kind of obstacles or barriers you might face, don't give up! Pursue what God called you to do with everything that is in you, and always remember that God is on your side. Rejoice and again I say rejoice.

ENDNOTES

1. The King James Version Full Life Study Bible
2. The King James Version Full Life Study Bible
3. Life Application Study Bible
4. Life Application Study Bible
5. Life Application Study Bible
6. How You Can Be Led By The Spirit Of God, Kenneth E. Hagin
7. Grace, Lewis Sperry Chafer
8. Exploring Revelation, John Phillips
9. Prayer, Richard J. Foster
10. The Power of Prayer, Norris Hall
11. Thru The Bible, J. Vernon McGee, Matthew through Romans
12. Christian Life Bible
13. Christian Life Bible
14. Signs Of The Times, M.R. DeHaan
15. The Rapture First, M. R. DeHaan
16. Revelation, M.R. DeHann
17. Thru The Bible, 1 Corinthians through Revelation, J. Vernon McGee
18. The Prayerful Spirit, James P. Gills, M.D.
19. If Not For The Grace Of God, Joyce Meyer